The November 2, 1984, issue of Scholastic's *Voice* magazine featured a young writer named Robyn Miller. The title of the issue was "A Handicapped Teenager's Own Story," and it featured stories, poems, and an essay by Robyn, a young girl who had found that writing was the best way for her to learn to live with illness. Robyn's disease, cystic fibrosis, is debilitating, progressive, and fatal. That issue of *Voice* was read by students all over the country, and many of those readers found a place in their hearts for Robyn. She got over 2,000 letters urging her to get well, congratulating her for hanging in there, and thanking her for sharing her story.

What follows is a collection of writings by Robyn. There are essays, stories, and poems; they are filled with laughter, tears, and wisdom. You'll get to know Robyn, and you'll understand why she made new friends wherever she went. This is a book about living, not dying; about fighting back, not giving in; about learning, about growing, about loving. This is Robyn's book.

**Other Point paperbacks
you will enjoy:**

Robyn's Book

A true diary
by Robyn Miller

SCHOLASTIC INC.
New York Toronto London Auckland Sydney

Some of the material in this book has appeared in other publications. "An Autobiography of Sorts," "The Teardown," "The Hidden Handicap," "Taking Leave," and "Steps" appeared in Scholastic's *Voice* magazine, November 2, 1984, Vol. 69, No. 5; "The Year" appeared in *Teen* magazine, February 1981; "The Year" and "Wedding Poem" appeared in *New Youth Connection*, November 1981; "Taking Leave" appeared in *With the Power of Each Breath, A Disabled Women's Anthology*, © 1985.

ISBN 0-590-42536-6

12 11 10 9 8 7 6 5 4 3 2   9/8 0 1 2 3/9

The author would like to express appreciation to the following people, who helped her so very much: Cora and Fred Miller, Ellen Miles, the staff of the Long Island College Hospital, the staff of the Office for Disabled Students at Barnard College, and my five favorite Voices: Niel Glixon, Sharon Linnea, Janet Galen, Jeff Derecki, and Shirley Ravich.

*This book is dedicated
to the memories of
Kenny Perkins,
Juliann Berkowitz,
Danny Ford,
Michael Malerba,
Keith Maddix,
and Akram Elfgeeh.*

Contents

Robyn's Book

A true diary

1.   Who I am

Once upon a time, two very excited new parents brought a much-loved, long-awaited baby daughter home from a hospital in Brooklyn, New York. They had wanted a child for many years, and in all that time alone as a couple, they dreamt many dreams. They imagined diaper changes, public schools, birthday parties. They imagined first steps, first words, first love. They imagined all the joys and pains that they could think of, but never did they imagine a baby who was not perfect, a child whose health they would have to guard all the years of her life. But fate threw them a curve, handed out to them the unimaginable. One year and one month after that tiny daughter came home, she was hospitalized for symptoms that included diarrhea and weight loss. The diagnosis was cystic fibrosis, and three lives were never again the same.

I am that baby girl, grown up. On March 27, 1985, I turned 21, no small feat when you consider that in 1964, my birth year, only one half of c.f. children lived to be 11. Today, thanks to new drugs, one half of the c.f. kids born live to be 20. I am ahead of the game, by any standard I can find, and all the more so because for my first 16 years I enjoyed something few c.f. kids experience — good health. Until I was a teenager I barely saw the inside of a hospital, never suffered from a lung infection, only rarely coughed. I considered myself lucky because I had two nice parents, two lovable dogs, lots of friends, a comfortable home. So much did I take my health for granted that if you'd asked me to count my blessings I would have put my stereo or my new three-speed bike on top of the list. I knew I had cystic fibrosis, knew it was progressive, even knew it was fatal. But the implications seldom hit home or made me worry. Illness and death might strike other people, but certainly not me.

On my parents' living-room wall there hangs a photo of that long-ago Robyn. She has light green eyes; shows a full, round face; and wears the biggest, brightest smile. Sometimes I stand in front of the photo and stare at her. Sometimes I do not recognize her as myself. The 16-year-old in the picture bears little resemblance to the skinny, club-fingered person c.f. has made me become. In all logic, I should envy that 16-year-old for all she had, from the hindsight of knowing all that she would later lose.

But I am not jealous of who I used to be.

Good health might have made the teenager that I was normal and happy, but it also left that teenager ignorant and shallow. The girl in that photo never knew what pain was, never understood what it meant to feel too hurt or disillusioned for tears. The girl in that photo never knew how stifling hospitals can be, and so she never appreciated the joy of waking up in her own bed. The girl in that photo never coughed horrible, choking coughs, and so she never realized how many perfect strangers will rush to help a person in trouble. The girl in that photo never did battle with an illness that wanted her life, and so she was less strong, less determined, less of a winner, than time would watch her become.

Now I am 21, and I hurt more than I used to. I do. I have days that are horrors, filled with gasps and chest aches, days when I wish I could be 16 and healthy once again. But I also have moments that overpower the pain, when I realize exactly how deep my luck runs. In the oddest way, the more ground cystic fibrosis takes from me, physically, the more I realize how much I've been given. This recognition has been hard-won, and even today I often forget to be grateful for a healthy stretch until I'm once again sick. But generally speaking, I don't sell life short anymore. I know how lucky I am to have the day, even if it must be spent on oxygen. Many, many times I have stood by the grave of a friend lost to cystic. There is very little I take for granted anymore.

And very little I don't thoroughly enjoy. Recently, filling out forms for college, I was stumped when asked to list my favorite hobbies. Pressed for time and space, I listed writing, reading, baby-sitting as my loves. But I would have liked to explain Robyn a little more thoroughly to the people reading those forms. I would have liked them to know that, practical though I may sometimes be, I have been known to spend whole days taking pictures of the flowers in my neighborhood park. I would have liked them to know that, just last year after a five-week hospitalization, I went out and touched the trees as though they were magic and might disappear. I would have liked them to know that I like losing myself in crowds, but I also like finding myself on paper, alone in my room, with a new pen and an old diary. I would have liked them to know that I liked what I knew of the Robyn they were meeting, but that I also didn't know her very well yet, because every time I'd get her down pat, she'd start to grow.

This book will introduce everyone to the ever-changing Robyn Miller. And to a few of my friends, whose spirit needs and deserves to be spread. And to the doctors and nurses who work with me and for me. And to a disease that can make you grow, if you're lucky, even while it makes you suffer, even while it threatens your life.

* * *

Every college student in a writing class experiences it. The professor wants you to write at your best. What's the easiest topic to assign for great results? Write an autobiography to share in class. It follows the old adage, doesn't it? Write about something you know.

Of course, every class surely has a Robyn in its midst, a person who doesn't quite know herself just yet, a person who's still enchanted by all she could be. A person whose autobiography comes out different from the others. I wrote this one a few years ago, but everything I said in it still applies.

Autobiography of Sorts

Needed — one autobiography of Robyn Miller, not too long and not too short, just your everyday accurate description, a Webster's definition of a person I've looked at in the mirror for 19 years and still have trouble figuring out. Include plenty of details; these will come in handy: If I'm busy telling how tall I am and how thin I am and how old I am no one will notice that I haven't told who I am, which is something I've been dying to know myself, so if you find out before I do, please let me know.

Due date — next Thursday, which is really curious, as if one can demand answers in seven days to questions I've been asking for years. I'll have a new assignment for you by next week, class, so please define yourselves quickly, let me know what you are and why you are so that I can grade you appropriately and then we can move on to other things.

What's an appropriate grade for a description of myself? Do I get an A for honesty if I tell how sometimes I spend hours happily by myself and how at other times when I'm with a whole bunch of my friends I get suddenly lonely? Do I get a good grade for exposing myself by telling about the crush I had on my seventh-grade biology teacher, or do I get a better grade if I'm discreet and don't mention how I spent two weeks on a diet counting every calorie religiously, only to give it all up at Häagen Dazs for a double scoop of maple walnut? Would I get points for self-assurance if I write that I think of myself as steadfast and reliable, and do I get graded down for poor self-esteem if I admit that I was terrified during all of my college interviews because I was suddenly positive that everyone else who applied was bigger, and brighter, and better?

What do I include in an autobiography, anyway? Should I tell about the people who have influenced my life? What if the people who have motivated me are just as normal and ordinary as I am? While everyone else is writing about the famous and inspiring people who have challenged and directed them, can I risk being laughed at by telling about the third-grade teacher who encouraged my first stabs at poetry? What will people say if

I write that I've been most inspired by my friend Brian, who is five years old and has leukemia and tells me he feels sorry for the doctor who gives him his spinal tap because "she looks so sad that she has to hurt me"? Will I be ridiculed in class if I choose my own mother for a heroine, because she once made it through a snowstorm that shut down most of New York to come visit me in the hospital when I was sick?

Do you think I can get away with giving pat answers? Can I identify myself by my height and weight and Social Security number, with hair length and eye color thrown in for good measure? When I was young I used to watch beauty contests on television, amazed at how the contestants managed to summarize their lives in two sentences. Miss Texas is Bobbie Jo Sinclair and she's five feet, six inches tall. She weighs 110 pounds, is an avid golfer, and she also enjoys tennis, canoeing, and reading Shakespeare. What does Robyn Miller enjoy? Who is this Miss Robyn of Brooklyn, anyway?

Sometimes I think I know her perfectly. When she sparkles and smiles I accept her as being happy, and when she suddenly bursts out crying for no apparent reason I can understand her tears. She makes sense to me thoroughly, I have her totally pegged, and there really isn't anything about her I can't grasp. Other times, when I see her unexpectedly in the mirror, or when I have to tell all about her in two paragraphs for a job

7

application, I am convinced that I don't know her very well at all. And those are the times when I am led to frustration, and I wonder how someone I have lived with so long can still be a stranger.

I doubt that I'll be able to describe Robyn by Thursday. Anything I write will be filled with inaccuracies, and nothing I write will be very consistent. Finding yourself is not an assignment you can easily deadline, and I suspect that years from now when English class has long been forgotten I'll still be looking in mirrors occasionally, searching for Robyn, and asking questions.

Perhaps I'll have more answers by then. For now, though, for Thursday, I can only promise to keep my eyes open and my ears sharp, and if I happen to discover her anytime soon, I'll let you know. But if by chance you discover Robyn before I do, drop me a line, okay? And tell Robyn I said we should get together soon and have lunch. I'd really like to meet her.

We have a lot to talk about.

2. Why I write

My friend Dave lives in a world of numbers. An engineering student in fact and by nature, he comes home from a whirlwind of math classes every day and writes mysterious-looking formulas for homework every night. His wardrobe includes a T-shirt with a complicated equation printed across it; he gives funny looks to people carrying copies of Shakespeare. Dave was meant for numbers.

I was not. I once asked Dave to explain his T-shirt to me, and he lost me somewhere between x^2 and -5. I offer to help him with his homework as a joke; we both burst out laughing, because I have more problems with the instructions than he has with the questions. I try to explain to him what I have against calculators and computers; the only charge I can issue with any sincerity is that they're both so unpoetic. I was not meant for numbers. I was meant for words.

My mother tells me that my love affair with the written word began early; in what was undoubtedly an effort to get an active three-year-old out of her hair, she introduced me to books. I probably haven't thanked her enough. She's probably regretted her decision more than once. Since the age of five I have practically lived in the library, devouring any book that looked good and a few that were awful. Books scatter like dust around the apartment in Brooklyn when I'm home; they turn up five at a time in the dining room, three in the living room, twelve on my bed. People always tease me that I've been reading for as long as I've been breathing. We have a joke in my family that, the way my lungs keep messing up, I actually read a good deal better than I breathe.

And reading, most naturally for me, led to writing. I have some second-grade poems hidden in a closet somewhere, proof that as long as I've been able, something always led me to write. The influences became more apparent as I grew up; my third-grade teacher gave lots of poetry assignments and tried to interest all her students in creative writing. Later teachers recruited any willing student for help with school newspapers, school literary magazines. Writing was fun, it was something I got praise for (very important to a child), and it was something I could never do quite right. I always wonder if this last wasn't the main attraction. Math assignments bored me quickly; you'd struggle to figure out an answer that was already well-known, that someone had found before you and that someone would find again after you. History assignments sometimes seemed a waste of time; the answers were already written down in a hundred books. But writing creatively was something that came uniquely from me, something that gave me my own pleasure and my own responsibility. Only Robyn Miller could put down on paper exactly how Robyn Miller saw the world. Only Robyn Miller could experiment with style and form and language before she felt things sounded best. Only Robyn Miller could struggle to improve something that she herself had created. It must have given a marvelous sense of power to the young person that I was, to know that so much could lie only in her hands.

And later on, of course, my need to write grew stronger because my reasons for writing changed. At 12 I was writing busily in a diary, a book that any 21-year-old will remember as her only friend the year she was 12. Frantic exclamations make up most of this diary (I saved it); either I was positively the ugliest-looking girl in seventh grade, or I was undeniably the girl most likely to win a certain boy's attention. That diary wasn't well-written by my present standards; it is in fact nothing short of incoherent at times. But it has honesty and candor, warmth and happiness, and I saved it because these are the memories that tell most about that 12-year-old.

A 12-year-old who soon became a 13-year-old, and then a 14-year-old, a full-fledged teenager. High-school poetry contests became open to me now, and the stakes were higher than ever before. I still struggled with words because I wanted them to sound best to me, still threw out 13 wrinkled copies of a poem that didn't quite capture my world on paper. But now other people were reading the finished products, the turnout of hour after hour on my bed with an old looseleaf note-book. I hoped then — still hope — that I wrote because I wanted to and needed to. The prizes were always treasured, and I am still proud of collecting quite a few. But what I treasured most, what kept me smiling all the way home from those contests, were the remarks from judges, teachers, principals, who had read the work of a teenager and taken it seriously. "You write as though you're helping the poem, and the poem is helping you," one judge told me. He was more intuitive than he probably realized.

Later, as a 16-year-old, I began a diary of my high-school years. I probably planned to write about school sports and debate teams, SATs and senior proms. What I ended up writing about was my very first hospital admission for complications of cystic fibrosis, an unforgettable initiation into a world that frankly terrified me. Anger, fear, shock — I can still read it in every page of that diary, the words of a young teenager just discovering her identity who suddenly had thrust upon her life a whole new and complicated set of variables. I was, in a word, lost, just

12

when I was sure I'd be finding myself some-
time soon. It took me at least two years to
regain my balance, and I used up every diary
entry and scrap of paper I could find in the
process.

November 3, 1980: Dr. Heffer thinks I should be in the hospital. What would I need a hospital for? Hospitals are for sick people only, aren't they? When did life get so out of control?

November 8, 1980: Everyone here has never been 16. No one remembers wanting privacy or a door to close the world on. Not one of these people ever spent tons of time on the telephone when they were my age. No one here ever *was* my age at all, or else they've forgotten.

November 9, 1980: I am NOT a baby because I'm scared of blood tests. I have never had test after test before. No one explains anything to me and I'm sick of it. When I ask them questions or act like I'm scared they tell me to act my age. If it weren't for a few of the nicer nurses, I'd go crazy. Today I had a nurse who made a point of knocking on my door before coming in. Maybe they're not all so bad after all.

November 10, 1980: A boy I already like named Danny seems to have adopted me. I am the resident fledgling, or so he thinks. Evidently I need to know how to check an IV, when to call a nurse, where the best cans of soda are kept. Funny how you meet a friend when you least expect to. He's only 11, but I can tell he's going to be a good friend.

He was. He was a good friend from the start. Danny led me through those first frustrating admissions, and then later, when I was already an old pro at everyday hospital life, he led me through a few gruesome times that were far from everyday. He led me through the death of the first two friends I lost to cystic. He helped me to talk about fears I might have left unvoiced. And always, in my best interest, he encouraged me to "write it down."

The first piece that follows is proof positive that "writing things down" helped me sort things out. In August, 1982, I was hit by lightning twice in a row, as first my wonderful Dr. Heffer died, and then cystic fibrosis won its battle with my friend Juliann. This last event took place while both Danny and I were patients in the hospital, an experience that I will never forget no matter how many tragedies c.f. throws my way. Imagine being down the hall from your sweetest friend, who is dying. Imagine how you'd feel if you had the same disease that was killing her, even as you took the pills and did the therapy that was no longer helping a friend to come out on top. Imagine being in the hospital at the very moment your friend's life ended. Before she turned 13, before you turned 17. Before you knew, or wanted to know, all the awful realities children are always shielded from. It was truth, cold and hurting and hitting home, and I needed all the paper I could find to deal with the horror. And so the first piece details every step of those two hard weeks in August and my own discovery of the way things are, the way things can be when cystic fibrosis gets the upper hand. And the second piece deals with a very simple explanation of harsh facts, an explanation written to any other child who suddenly finds him- or herself occupying a strange adult world.

Finally, the last piece is also an attempt to sort things out. During my last few years as a teenager there was a terrible movement brewing in New York to tear down some beautiful landmark theaters. I had friends in a Broadway show nearby, and on Saturdays as I walked to their theater I would pass picketers protesting the proposed demolition. All of them looked as though they considered the teardown a political issue, but once, only once, I saw a man who saw something marvelous in those old theaters. A stagehand, perhaps, who loved that particular building, or just an old-timer who preferred pretty old buildings to smart new skyscrapers. And I wrote "The Teardown" for this man I never really met, from the point of view of a young girl who is just learning to question her right to have her own point of view. And I questioned then, as I question now, rereading the story, what it means to go forward, whether this society of ours isn't all wrong about progress. I can tell you myself that progress isn't always all it's cracked up to be. I have a progressive disease, you know.

August

Dear Juliann,

I hate August. Even now, so many years after August first hurt me, I feel myself bracing quietly in late July, stiffening and wondering what other tricks August might yet have up her sleeve. I take nothing for granted. August used to mean only another month of vacation, four weeks when surely the most disturbing part of my life would be sunburn. But two years ago, when August ended, my entire world was thrown off base. I expected more from a month I used to fill up with shopping sprees and barbecues, and for the rest of that autumn something in me stung with disbelief. That heart attacks could spring up and rob us of a doctor we loved — yes, I could expect that. That cystic fibrosis, never satisfied with the masses of children it has already smothered, could come after another victim — yes, I could expect that, too. That you should die while I watched . . . I was as prepared as years of crying for you and endless long talks with doctors could make me. But for it all to descend in August, on hot summer days meant for jogs and swims and body life. . . . Do you understand, Juli, why something still hurts me in late July?

What were you doing the first weeks of that August, Juli? Did you cry the way I did when Dr. Heffer died? I never had a chance to tell you about how his life ended for me, with a phone call from his secretary while we were vacationing upstate. Vacationing, Juliann, I still thought August was for vacations, and then the phone rang and by the time I put down the receiver a 19-year friendship had ended. "A heart attack," Roseann told me. His last one of three. Finishing the man who went back to work a few short weeks after past heart troubles, because, he told my mother, "There are kids of mine sick, and they need me." He was always conscientious, and he had a unique capacity to quietly put up with every rotten mood this particular "kid" of his could send his way. Three days after he died, I was as obnoxious as ever, my quiet hours of crying replaced by anger at God, fate, luck, and any other force that might have had a hand in robbing me of the one doctor who always thought of me as a person first and a lung disease second. I missed him, Juliann. Were you hurting, too? Did your mother manage to say something that got you over sorrow quickly? Or did you spend the last few weeks of your life hurting for someone you'd see again too soon?

I know what you expected of that August, Juliann. I know you believed August would bring you nothing more exciting than visits to cousins and games with the new cat. I know you were not waiting for trouble of any kind, not even on the August day when your troubles began. I know this because, months after your troubles were over, I went to your house to visit your mother, and there on the

17

living room floor were your shoes. Not shoes your mom was boxing up to throw away. Your shoes, the ones you'd decided not to wear that day to the hospital, kept in the same spot on the floor where you must have tossed them aside just before you left. You picked other shoes to wear that morning, and when you got to the hospital you were as impish and Juliann as ever, insisting to Debbie that you most certainly were not sick enough to stay in the hospital more than 10 days. And just a few weeks later you were gone entirely, Juliann, except for your toys and your books and the shoes you left in your living room that August day before you died.

I marked a record of that August, Juli. I followed your footsteps to the hospital just a few days later, plagued by the lung infection cystic fibrosis sends me every so often to remind me who's boss. By the time I got near you, I knew that lung infections were the least of our problems, and I spent the next two weeks lying in wait for what c.f. planned next. And aching to give you use of my own deadly, diseased lung tissue. And remembering — at rare intervals, when I was not so numb as to forget — that I was on *vacation*. And wondering, on August 28 when it all ended, if summers would ever feel quite the same to me again, if for the rest of my life thinking of August would mean thinking of two tiny unused shoes on a living-room floor.

* * *

Cans of soda and Garfield pictures on Intensive Care walls, drawn by a physical therapist and proof that this alarm that I feel is ludicrous. No child who asks for her favorite soda can be dying. No child who, oxygen mask notwithstanding, sits up and tells me softly about exactly what Garfield is doing in each picture, could possibly be the cause of this fear in my heart. Curses on cystic fibrosis for letting me think for even one second that this child is in danger.

"How's she doing?" I bombard Marcia, the first nurse I see, before my bags are unpacked. My mother has talked me into this admission on the pretense of visiting Juliann, who is, by her mother's deliberately calm testimony, not so bad. I packed my bags slower after Arlene delivers this news. I packed my bags in record time after calling Dr. Doyle to tell her I need a bed. "Good. I was going to ask you anyway to visit Juliann." She was going to ask me anyway to visit Juliann? This same woman, who encourages, threatens, and cajoles her patients into developing a life away from the hospital, was going to ask me to visit Juliann? I am in the hospital within the hour by the clock, shaking with anxiety from every word Dr. Doyle left unsaid.

People do not get worse in hospitals. I tell this hotly to the nurse who brings me progressively worse news on Juliann. People come to hospitals to grow well and go home. People in hospitals sometimes flounder for a few shaky days, but then some modern-day wizard comes up with just the right antibiotics to save the day. People do better and better in hospitals, and any minute now Juliann will turn around and follow suit.

Sure, Robyn, and nothing bad ever happens in August.

Nothing in the world can hurt like my ignorance. During the day I sneak looks at the manuals by the nurses' station, memorizing the definitions of the medical terms I've heard in Intensive Care. Lung disease. Heart disease. What is hurting my Juliann? Dr. Doyle calls me aside and I give her a medical quiz, complete with the very strong implication that she is not doing all that science trained her to do. I alternately suggest stronger antibiotics, more physical therapy, a respirator, a lung transplant. With whose lungs? With your lungs. With my lungs! Who cares whose lungs? I stop myself when I realize that this person I am yelling at, with the stethoscope complete with koala bears and raccoons, would probably accept in a minute if she could only trade places with the 12-year-old in I.C.U.

"What did Dr. Doyle tell you?" asks Danny, my best c.f. friend from the hospital, lately my best friend, period; the only boy I know who accepts my fears and anger with fears and anger of his own. Danny of the Danny-and-Juliann twins, as I call them in my heart. Born two months apart to different families, sharing the same freckles, the same grade in school, the same monstrous disease. No kind words for cystic fibrosis from me, not today, not after the session with a doctor who can't possibly save the other half of the Danny-Juli twins.

"She told me her lungs were filled with too much mucus for her to breathe. I told her, why can't they open her up and shovel out the damn mucus? And she told me it would grow back, and Juli wouldn't survive the surgery anyway." Danny nods at the answers to the questions he probably learned years ago not to ask. Sickly from birth, Danny has gone this route with other c.f. friends time and again. If he lives — for as long as he lives — he can expect to lose even more friends. And lately my comfort, inexcusably small though it is, has been the mere fact of Danny's presence, the fact that this one small, 12-year-old, freckle-faced boy with the cough has lost friend after friend after friend, and he has survived.

I write little of what I do here, because I do little. I spend the days with therapists, trying to keep my own rotted lungs from rotting more, and with nurses who seem more bent and determined to feed me pills than they've been in years. I notice the strangest pattern now: the insistence by the staff to get me well as fast as possible. I don't think it's a question of my being here while my friend is so sick, although certainly they are trying to clear the hospital of cystics, and have already sent home the Tirados. No, it's more a question of people here needing a success story, needing to see that the therapy and the antibiotics still work for someone, if not for Juliann. They stay closer to me than ever before, this staff, wanting to be with at least one kid who doesn't wake up blue in the face every morning; who doesn't hover in and out of consciousness the way Juliann now seems to; who will, with any luck at all, walk out of this hospital again and again.

Will Juliann not walk out of this hospital? I visit her every day in I.C.U., taking two minutes by the doorway to paste the smile on my face and know it's secure. "Hi, Juli," I tell her. And stand grateful for the closed eyes. Her eyes are only partially open these days, and her face drips with sweat that her mother wipes away every minute of every hour. I ask a nurse about the sweat and she tells me Juliann is overheated. Juliann is working so hard to breathe that she sweats. Juliann is concentrating so hard on doing something almost everyone else in the world takes for granted that she lies here with closed eyes, her mind turned in within herself. And I stand with her, foolishly holding the stuffed frog she used to love, grateful for the closed eyes that cannot see the tears form in my own.

Donald does my physical therapy this afternoon. Physical therapy is done on every patient with cystic fibrosis every day, until the patient is so hopelessly ill that therapy won't help. Donald is my therapist this time around, a tall guy with gray hair, quick to joke and to make fun of all the stuffed animals on my bed. He hasn't smiled all week. "Are you doing Juliann's therapy?" I ask Donald. "No." "Is Joanne doing Juliann's therapy, then?" Quiet. "No." "Is anyone doing Juliann's therapy?" Damn my cracked voice. "No, Rob." And I cry, my first real tears of recognition, when he leaves. There is nobody doing Juliann's therapy. Over and over, the same waves of pain. There is nobody doing Juliann's therapy.

Her mother lies to the two of us every day. She comes to my room and I drop the phone, turn off the TV, and we sit while I listen to dreams that won't come true. "When she comes home, you have to come over and see the cat." Arlene's voice is steady. I keep wondering how much of this fantasy she believes.

I keep wondering how much of this fantasy I believe. I sit near Juliann's bed today for only one or two minutes, and in that time I concoct more lies than a politician. "Wait till you see what we do on your birthday," I tell Juli. "It's only two months away, you know, we'd better get started planning now." And Arlene nods, willing to put up with whatever antics two teenagers come up with, willing Juliann in her heart to leave this place and turn 13.

The nights are worst, because at night we

keep vigil. Something in me — something silly and irrational but insistent — tells me that if I go to bed Juliann will die. If I relax, let myself drop off, something will steal her from me. So I stay awake, on guard, all night. And Danny's been spending the nights awake with me. Always a late-night movie fan, he is up long after every sick person I know, and now he spends his time in my chair. We play Monopoly together, watch the news if it's not too boring. I read him Garfield and he giggles. I laugh at his laughter. It always surprises me that in the middle of this nightmare we can laugh.

I ask my mother to bring me the candle Juliann gave me for my birthday. I want to keep it on the table near my bed. Someday I am going to clean my room of junk, but I want to keep that candle forever. In the shape of a beagle holding a birthday cake. With the sweet touch of Juliann.

Tomorrow Debbie Tirado turns 11. One of the strongest cystics I've seen, bright blond hair flying from a body that somehow manages to grow and keep weight on. No small feat. I've lost five pounds myself this week. No time to care.

I call her from the hospital to ask her what presents she wants most. I am willing to buy her a great deal this year. I am more like the nurses and doctors than I thought: willing to do anything for this cystic kid who is not dying down the hall.

I stay awake all night tonight. Listening to the sounds and imagining that all footsteps head toward Juliann. And rereading this journal, for proof positive that there ever was a healthy, happy Juli, who liked lunches in restaurants and playing with her hamster. Thinking of her, I cannot help but compare her to the girl down the hall, the one whose mother now spends night and day by her side. And in the darkness, when I know how little Juliann has left, I think . . . forgive me what I think, Juliann, in the darkness.

And it starts at 8 A.M. The latest reports on her, complete with tales of high fevers. The quick talk with her grandmother, who looks this morning like she's lived too long. The quick shout from Arlene, who tells a resident that they need him *right now*. And then the run down the hall, where I can huddle in my room, because, God forgive me, Juliann, I cannot watch you die.

Yesterday I held your hand in the Unit. A bag of bones in the bed, all effort on breathing, and I thought you did not have the strength to make a sound. And then, as I moved out to leave, you gripped my hand tighter, one squeeze of a power that took all gathered at your bed by surprise. Unconscious you may have been most of the week, but no one will ever convince me you weren't saying good-bye. Good-bye, Robyn. Hello, Robyn. I'm glad you were my friend. I wish it weren't like this. . . . And I stand by the Unit now, with my nurse Eileen, thinking of all you meant to tell with your hand in my own.

And after it's all over, they let me see you — early on, when I am only slightly crying. I walk past nurses sitting quietly at the Unit desk. They turn away from me now, and I understand. Later, when I am lying in Intensive Care myself, needing help, they will run to my side and never let me alone. But now they cannot look at me, healthy, with all the naked pain in my eyes. What's it like to lose a friend to the same disease still waiting for you? These people who loved you, who love me yet, cannot bear to imagine.

So still. So irrefutably, for always, still. I have never seen a dead body before. "You can touch her," they tell me. I brush back some of your hair, feel the pulse in your head quiet. Near you all week, I had thought of you as being dead when you were alive. But you realize, when it's gone, how full of life a human body is. So still, Juli, and for the rest of my time I won't forget it, how sweet and how peaceful you manage to look even now in all your stiff stillness.

Walking to the Unit to see my favorite nurses, to share their sodas. And glance after unbearable glance at where you died. Night after night.

A few days after your funeral I leave for college, freshman year. I shut my hospital door knowing that I am going off to make new friends. But I am leaving one of them behind forever.

Sometime in November I realize I have gone the whole day without thinking of Juli. When my friends ask me who the pretty girl is in the photo by my bed I give them her name. When I call Arlene back in Brooklyn, we talk about the cat, my classes, her new job. When I forget about summer I can almost have fun.

And when I still miss her I remember the picture Danny crayoned for I.C.U. that August, the one we put by her bed in hopes she'd know it was there. The one with the three Garfields hugging. Captioned, "Friendship goes on and on."

The Explanation

One day, when the earth was busy and all the people were rushing about, God looked down on the world He had made. He looked at the forests, the oceans, and the fields. He looked at big cities and small towns. But mostly He looked at the children, because God especially loves children.

And His eye took Him to a little girl's house. This little girl wasn't running, or jumping, or playing. Instead she was lying face down on a bed, letting her mother do the therapy that sometimes helped her to breathe.

And God said, "This is a child I love especially. She cannot run without becoming short of breath. She does not spend a day in which she is rid of her cough. But she is brave and she is loving, and I am going to help her."

And an angel asked God, "What will You do for her?"

And God replied, "I will call her Home. I will take her to Heaven where she can breathe without pain. I will care for her Myself because this little girl is very special to Me."

But God knew He had many other children to look after, and He would need some help in caring for this girl. And He thought, "Before I call her Home, I need to call Home someone else. I need to find someone who loves this girl dearly, who weeps as I do when children struggle to breathe. I need to find someone kindly and wise, someone who is dedicated to children everywhere. I must find someone very special."

And again God searched the cities and the towns. He looked on farms and fields all over the world, and at last His eye caught a hospital in Brooklyn. There He saw a kindly, aging doctor. He watched the doctor examine each child with love, and He saw the concern the doctor had for the children who were not well. And God knew then He had found the right helper, and on a quiet August day He called Home Dr. Ernest Heffer.

And then God looked once more at the little girl, who was beginning to show signs of lung infection. And God said, "Let her not struggle to breathe anymore. Here in Heaven there is no lung disease. She will breathe and run and play like other children. And she will have a doctor who loved her to take special care of her. Yes, she is ready to come to Me now."

And just a bit later, Juliann Berkowitz went Home.

The Teardown

A Short Story

The day of the teardown is a damp slice of May. My father dresses with awkward care, the new suit stiff in his calloused palms. Downstairs, he is answering my mother's chatter, his voice slow and proud in response to her chirps. She is nervous. He isn't. He is the hero of today and knows it; some days my mother complains about his long hours as a construction foreman, some days my brother and I grimace at his mortar-stained jeans, but today he is a hero and everyone knows it. My father is in charge of the teardown of the Keller.

I braid my hair carefully and try to imagine the theater. I have seen it only once. It is small and fussy, with elaborately designed doors and windows, and three marble columns by the front entranceway. It is one story high — "Not making use of the sky!" my father says — and inside there are plush carpets that cost a fortune to clean. My father told me the Keller seats 300 people. My auditorium at high school seats 450.

I finish tying my braids and I go to my closet. Construction sites are dirty but I want to dress up, knowing that today is important to my father. When I was little I liked going with my dad and my brother to vacant lots, watching Daddy show important-looking plans to his workers. Sometimes we would go back to the same site months later and a building would have risen like magic in the lot. My father would take us inside and show us shiny new elevators and apartments, and I would marvel that he could make such wonderful things come from the dirt.

When I walk down the stairs my mother sees me and beams, nodding approval at my skirt and my neatly combed hair. My brother is wearing a tie I've never seen, and I wonder if this is my mother's doing, too. Todd is the type of boy who works computers and watches space shots on television; his room is filled with rocket models and books on astronomy. Ties are alien to Todd. "He's a busy boy," my father argues when my mom complains about Todd's clothes. "So he can't be bothered dressing up like you want. And it's good that he's so busy and active in everything. You want him to be a go-getter, don't you?" *Go-getter* is a word my father uses a lot. "You can be anything you want to, do anything you want," he always tells me and Todd. "Maybe in the old days everything was set and fixed, but now there are new opportunities every day!" Another word he uses a lot is *progress*. "Progress is a wonderful thing!" he always says, and something far-away and exciting in his voice makes me believe him.

It is progress that I think about on the way to the theater. My father is driving and my mother is fiddling with the radio, trying to find a station reporting the news. The media have been broadcasting reports on the Keller all week, on the teardown and the apartment houses going up in its place. The *Daily Herald* printed sketches of the buildings on Friday and my father showed them proudly to us at dinner. "Lots of room," he noted, pointing to floor after floor of apartments. "Good solid steel, thick glass, everything sturdy and new."

The *Daily Herald* agrees with my father. "The Gold apartment complex scheduled to go up at the site of the James Keller Theater gives new meaning to the word *skyscraper*," my mother read. "Accommodating several thousand people, it will include two separate buildings of 25 stories each. Work on the complex should entail steady employment of hundreds of construction workers, and won't be complete for at least 10 months." I hear the numbers and figures repeated until I know them by heart, but after dinner I sneak the newspaper upstairs with me anyway. In my room with the door closed I stare at the sketches, looking at the long lean lines of the buildings. I try to imagine how much space those buildings will cover, how much sky. Even on paper they looked imposing.

My father drives quickly through the morning traffic and parks the car on a side street half a block from the Keller. Two cranes are in place by the theater entrance, and men with hardhats and messy jeans are talking to other men who wear business suits and broad smiles. My parents leave the car and walk toward a man with a sheaf of papers in his hand who greets my father effusively and shows him the papers he's holding. I look around for something to do; sometimes the construction workers bring their children and I talk to them, but today there are only men and my brother has disappeared. I walk from the car closer and closer to the cranes and when I look up I am standing in front of the Keller.

I don't remember its being so small. It squats in the center of the street, close to the sidewalk, and does not seem to take up any space at all. The marble columns cluster by the doorway and I go closer to look at the thick brown door. By the side of the door there are etchings of flowers and leaves, and the date the cornerstone was laid is engraved in tiny roman numerals. I trace the pattern of a leaf and think how pretty the design is. I never noticed the flowers and leaves before.

Someone has left the door partly open. In a few minutes when the cranes are ready the workers will come with blockades and my father will call to his men to finish roping off the sidewalk. I glance around at the construction men who are still gathered in groups talking, and I open the door quickly and let myself in.

It is dark in the Keller. The plush carpets are spongy underneath my sandals and I make my way slowly down an aisle. I like the cushiony feeling against my feet. I sink into a seat five rows from the stage and I like the soft, worn-out velvet against my back and my shoulders. I smooth down the velvet on the arms of the chair and look at the stage. It would be comfortable watching a show from a place like this.

I try to imagine this theater on opening night. I don't have much material to imagine with; I have been to the theater only once or twice in my life, and always on a Saturday afternoon when tickets come cheaper. The last time I saw a show I was 12; my mother took me when Todd was away at camp for the summer. My father didn't come; I wanted him to, but he said he had a brand new tennis racket to try out and he wasn't about to pay that kind of money to sit still. I never remember him being stingy with money, but all my life he's been paying to be part of the action, taking us ice skating and back-packing and buying us jogging shoes for our birthdays. My mother bought me all my jigsaw puzzles when I was little, and the summer I was nine I sat for hours working them through. Sometimes my father would bounce through the living room where I was sitting, and he'd look with a funny expression at the table in front of me with all the puzzle pieces spread out. "I'm running down to the corner for a little jog," he would say. "How about giving me a run for my money?" Sometimes I agreed and went to change into sneakers, but most of the time I said no, thank you, and stayed in the house with my puzzles. I knew he mentioned those times to my mother at night when they were lying in bed, because I could hear them talking if I went to get a glass of water. "Hell of a way to spend the summer, don't you think? No, I don't mean there's something wrong with being quiet, but what's up with that kid, anyway? Where's her get-up-and-go?"

I wonder what my father is doing now, while his daughter is doing what he once said he wouldn't pay money for, sitting still in a theater and watching the curtains. They are thick red curtains, the kind you still see in old houses, the kind they tie up all day in long gold cord. My grandmother had curtains like that in her bedroom. They were heavy and forest green and warmed the room like a sun, and we sold them after my grandmother died. I was eight and thought we should keep the curtains for our living room, but Daddy said that cotton curtains are more practical and he explained it until I understood. I wonder if my father has seen the curtains in the Keller. I wonder if my father has been inside the Keller, ever.

Someone is making noises on the sidewalk. I can hear voices faintly, bouncing down the aisle and breaking the quiet, and I stand up and walk in the dim light to the door. The brown door opens from the outside before I reach for the doorknob, and I jump when a man coming in nearly knocks me down. "Christ, I didn't see you — what are you doing here, kid?" I stare at him dumbly, squinting my eyes. It takes a moment to get used to the sunlight flooding in. "Well, gee whiz, kid, you better get out of here now. I'm just about to go help set up a blockade. Had an idea I should check in here first, for people. Looks like I was right." The bulky man in jeans follows me out of the entrance and shuts the door before I have a chance to look back.

Outside, the sidewalk is white with sunlight and the Keller makes a squat shadow under my feet. I glimpse my father behind a blockade near the gutter, standing by my mother and looking every inch a hero. I walk toward them and notice that a reporter is headed their way, too, followed by a photographer who has been snapping pictures of the Keller and the cranes. My father sees me and extends his hand out to me proudly. I stop to wipe my hands on a tissue before I take his. I can still feel the velvet from the theater seat on those hands.

The reporter gets to my father before I do and is shooting questions at him by the time I reach his side. The photographer drags my parents away for a picture and I am left standing by the blockades, alone, facing the Keller. I stare at the theater's marble columns and I think about the velvet. I stare at the brown door and think about the leaves on that door.

I can hear the reporter talking quickly to

my father. He is asking my father questions and listening to every word my father says. I used to listen to my father like that — when I was little.

"Can you tell my readers, sir, if you have any qualms about this project? Don't you have any misgivings about tearing down the old to put up the new?"

I am still looking at the Keller when my father answers. "Oh, not at all, sir, not at all," he says. "It's like I always tell my children. Progress is a wonderful thing, you know? Progress is a wonderful thing."

3. Differences

One of my youngest friends has cancer. A bubbly little girl, she bounces into people's lives with both feet, unless she's using those feet to chase other kids down hospital halls or to prance from room to room showing off her new dolls. Sometimes I doubt her ability to stay still for more than a minute, but I never doubted her ability to make lots of friends. And then one day last year, as her chemotherapy treatments approached an end, my little friend and I were sitting happily in the hospital, listing all of the wonderful things that she could do once her cancer ordeal was finally over. I had expected her to list among the things she looked forward to most an end to feeling nauseous from the medicines and an end to hospital visits. But I was startled at what headed her list. "Once I'm through with all this treatment, I won't be bald or skinny or always out of school. There won't be anything wrong with me anymore. I'm going to be just like the others."

Just like the others. I don't suppose that bounciness, or youth, or even the most outgoing, resilient personality stops a person from wanting to blend right in, from fearing inside that some difference, be it baldness or skinniness or a hacking cough, will totally and for always set him apart from everyone else. For some of us, of course, there are tangible differences for people to point their fingers at; my little friend had gone to school and played outside many times with no hair on her head and the foolish whispers of strangers behind her back. Others of my friends live in the world every day with similar long-term differences — a wheelchair, a speech impediment, a face discolored by blood disease.

At the other end of the spectrum, some of my friends with Cooley's Anemia appear "normal," yet must balance their show of "normalcy" with the knowledge that they do in fact have a serious and incurable sickness. Unfortunately, people with cystic fibrosis often end up coping with both extremes — dealing with the comments of onlookers who assume a fierce cough to mean a contagious cold, while dealing with the inner knowledge that a sickness far worse than any cold is at work here. Singled out for stubby fingers, for blue lips, for a skinny frame, and for that famous cough, I sometimes want to return insult for insult, even while finding it ironic that I am not singled out for the aspect of my illness that really makes me most different from other 21-year-olds — its terminal na-

ture. People who see me as different, who believe me to be in the throes of a bad case of bronchitis or a bout with the flu, often amuse me in a sad sort of way because they don't know the half of it. I am a person subjected to a chronic illness, a hidden disability, and so the worst of my differences cannot be guessed at by a stranger.

I have never been "like the others." Even when I was younger and healthier, I showed symptoms of my sickness: a thin body, a protruding stomach from digestive problems, a tendency to sweat a lot in the summertime. I don't recall too many stares resulting from these symptoms, because, after all, any little kid can have a pot belly and get perspired. What I do recall provoking questions was the demands that c.f. made, even then, on my time and my life-style. I was the kid who took pills before eating her lunch at school. I was the kid who could not order the chocolate ice cream cone from the Good Humor man. I was the kid who slept in a mist tent at night. I was the kid who, every so often, missed school to go to the doctor and get checked out. Looking back, I would think that all these "differences" would have hurt me terribly, would have caused the other kids to make the kind of cruel remarks little children (and ignorant adults) seem to specialize in. But I cannot remember more than a handful of taunts. I cannot remember a specific incident where I was picked on or avoided for all the ways c.f. changed me from the norm. And so I do not remember being underconfident or self-deprecating because of my sickness. Insecurities I assuredly had, but they stemmed more from the usual classroom squabbles and less from cystic fibrosis. As I've grown older and seen more of the ways of curious strangers, I have come to realize that I was unusually and blessedly lucky to have my medical problems cause me so little trauma as a child.

I like to believe now that one of the reasons I escaped feeling different was the matter-of-fact way in which my parents treated my illness. When I was very small, I spent a great deal of time with a group of little friends whose mothers joined mine at the neighborhood park. These kids were naturally curious about "why Robyn takes pills and I don't," but when they asked questions they were given answers that they could understand, answers that did not make "Robyn" sound like the neighborhood weirdo. Because their parents were also all filled in about c.f., my friends found that they could get information not only from my mother but from their very own parents. Most of my friends thus grew up with a better knowledge of c.f. and a far more casual attitude toward sickness than most adults have. In fact, since even a disease pales for little kids in the face of such immediate concerns as whose turn it is to ride the swing, little attention was paid to my sickness beyond a few well-meant questions. When attention was paid, it was more often to give support than to hurt or tease — I

41

still remember all the times my friends ordered vanilla ice cream cones because I couldn't eat chocolate and they didn't want to make me feel bad. I was different, and I knew it, but I was not made to feel concerned.

And of course, I didn't know yet about the more serious differences. I did not know that c.f. was fatal. I did not know that right now, this very minute, there were c.f. kids exactly my age, stuck in hospitals — or worse, in cemeteries — even as I played with my friend Sharon on the sliding pond. There is a great debate going on today about how much information chronically ill children should be given about their diseases, about which facts will help them cope with their sickness and which facts will only foster in them a sense that they are unworthy, not like "the others." When I was a child, my parents solved this debate for themselves by deciding to give me, at every age, as much information as I could grasp. My mom remembers making this decision consciously, after a fellow c.f. parent told her that his teenaged c.f. daughter handled her sickness poorly because her folks had kept her illness a dark secret for many years. I probably benefited from these parents' mistakes a great deal, since my vocabulary even as a three-year-old included such medical terms as "postural drainage," spoken effortlessly and with very little self-consciousness. But of course, a three-year-old who is ready to cope with the names of her treatments is not necessarily ready to cope with the knowledge that in spite of these treatments, c.f. might end in early death. Looking back, I was probably shielded from this knowledge until I was at least 10 or 11, and then I was only gradually introduced to the idea that some c.f. children were not doing as well as I was. Say what you will about protecting children from distressing news, I still think that openness is the best possible policy in accustoming a child to any of her differences, including a limited life span. I do not recall any one moment when I "realized" that my life expectancy would not be the same as my friends'. I grew up with this knowledge, and all the better for me in the long run. Never, never once, did I feel different from the others because I had just unearthed some terrible, mysterious news about my future.

My parents probably assumed that discussing my sickness openly would help me develop greater sensitivity and become a reasonable, well-adjusted adult. They were rewarded for their efforts by early signs that I was unusually touched by other people's problems; but when I entered adolescence they met plain evidence that I was far from well adjusted. My first hospitalization at age 16 revealed that I was angry, upset, and very poorly equipped to deal with all the worst aspects of cystic fibrosis. Every member of my hospital staff will testify that they were dealing with a stubborn, sullen girl, a girl prone to ripping out IV needles and screaming at doctors without reason, a girl who was frightened but who covered up her fears with rage and plain obnoxious behavior. Looking back, I can understand most of this behavior, even if I cannot excuse it. I had grown up thinking I was perfectly normal. I had grown up believing that hospitalizations and differences and death were situations other c.f. patients would have to cope with, but not me. I had expected to be a 16-year-old just like the other 16-year-olds. And here I was, with a disease that had finally caught up to me, time and time again in the hospital! It looked like I was back at square one, with a whole new set of differences to adjust to and a whole new image of myself to accept.

The staff gave up. It was too hard trying to understand the problems of a 16-year-old, and too time-consuming to talk with a girl who was as likely to yell at you as she was to listen. My mother threw up her hands. "You're just the same as before," she frequently told me, but she was a mother, after all, and what 16-year-old believes her mother? I was as ready to give up on myself as the others, as willing to spend the rest of my life in bed convinced I was abnormal. And then there came influence from a group no one had counted on — my friends. My doctors had forgotten that one word from a peer is worth 10 from a professional. My parents had forgotten that all their speeches about living as normally as possible could never equal the movie dates, the concert tickets, the long phone calls my friends included me in —

still. I had forgotten myself that my friends were more concerned with how much I cared about them than how much I coughed. Looking back, I feel foolish for having wasted so much time concentrating on my differences, but remain grateful for all those teenagers who saw in me all that was gloriously ordinary.

And so these days, I figure that c.f. won't set me apart if I believe it won't. More and more, I am keeping a good perspective, bearing in mind that I have more likenesses to, than differences from, the others, even while remembering that there are plenty of other kids with c.f. whose fingers are stubbier and whose coughs are harsher than my own. Some of this positive thinking comes from spending time with friends like Jenny, who prods me good-naturedly into going for long walks; and Sara, who asks me about my writing before she asks me about my health; and Nicole, who gives me such wild hugs when we meet at the hospital that you'd think we were having a party instead of having more IV treatments. Some of this positive thinking comes from hospital staff members, many of whom quiz me more thoroughly about my latest exam grades than about my latest lung infection. And some of this positive thinking comes from me, from the new attitudes I've developed about which parts of me count and which parts of me don't.

The stories that follow reflect those new attitudes. The first piece deals with a little boy with motor disabilities, who with any luck will inherit more of his sister's sensitivity than his father's indifference. The initial idea for "The Architect" came from my friendship with Kenny, a c.f. teenager with whom I played basketball in the hospital hallways many years ago. Kenny was terribly lung-damaged when I knew him, quite obviously dying, and it took all his energy to shoot those balls. But I gave Kenny the respect I'd normally save for a Wilt Chamberlain, because with every basket he made he scored a point for living "like the others." The second piece focuses on a mentally impaired youngster, who knows that he's fine just the way he is until society tells him otherwise. Although I have totally reworked the storyline, "Brian" results from a conversation I had with the mother of my real-life little friend, Brian, who waged a fight against cancer with all the strength of a small Superman. When Brian's mother expressed concern that his bald head might elicit cruel remarks from the other schoolchildren, I began to think and then to write about how poorly we socialize our children to deal with someone who is "different."

Fortunately, there are exceptions to this rule. Not long ago, I visited a tiny friend in the hospital, who had recently been freed from an assortment of tubes that seemed to cover his whole body. When I asked him if everyone had made a fuss over his new appearance, he wrinkled his nose. "Robyn," my friend said in disgust, "people like me for me!"

46

The Architect
A Short Story

You are nine the day I teach you to print. I teach you because Father is busy huddled over his plans, making strokes that coax skyscrapers into neat, ruled life. On his desk is a protractor with complicated dials. I have to search awhile for a number-two pencil.

On white typing paper I draw you an A. I try to show you the triangular sides, the line that pierces them in the center. It is not easy. The lack of attention span that frustrates your special ed. teachers, that sends you from crayons to blocks to toy cars on rainy Saturdays, also keeps you from watching the way my hands move. But I hand you the pencil anyway and you begin.

Your tiny spastic fingers wrap around the yellow lead. I have a sudden memory of your first painting in kindergarten, splashes of red and yellow without any obvious shape. You told Father proudly it was a house and he said, "That's nice. But wouldn't it be better if the windows were straighter?" Wanting to help, he had only hurt. You held back the tears but later I found the picture crumpled in your garbage can.

Sweat is forming on your thumb and index finger. You grip the pencil too tightly, to prevent it from sliding. Laboriously, you print the first line of the triangle, bearing the pencil down heavily to make thick, crooked marks. Your brows are furrowed and I see

creases in your forehead. I try to remember
if my own tries at printing took this much
effort. I think of Father in the next room,
sketching buildings with ease.

I leave to get milk and I bring you a glass.
But you shake your head imperceptibly, in-
tent on your work. You have reached the apex
of the A and your fingers make their slow way
downward. I can see the start of a blister near
the base of the thumb. I think of how good
milk tastes when I break from homework, and
almost press the cool glass forcibly in your
palm. But I stop because I cannot compare
your efforts to mine. When have I ever
worked this hard on homework?

Father is making rustling sounds in the
den. I hear him clicking off the lamp and
shuffling paper into piles. I know that he is
done and that he will place his drawings
in an orderly pile on his desk. Tomorrow his
boss will admire his exactness and soon his
even lines will be transformed into brick.

You raise the pencil from the paper at the
base of the A, scrutinizing your work before
you begin the center line. Splinters of pencil
are fraying near your hand, forming ugly red
sores on your fingers and palm. I remember
Father's protractor with its steel silver point
and wonder if his work ever caused him any
pain.

Father heaves as he stretches to pull his
jacket from the coat rack. He calls from the
doorway that he is bringing the plans to the

office. You look up for the first time from your work to yell good-bye.

Good-bye! You are going to discuss architecture with the men at your firm. And you are leaving behind an architect who must struggle to design an A.

Your breath is heavy when you lay down the pencil. On a grimy piece of paper, yellow with sweat, there is an A. It is bedraggled and moistened from your hot breath, but still an A. Sweat dampens your hands and your forehead is gleaming slightly, but there is no film to hide your smile that comes from being *able*. I glance at the letter that was printed because you are strong and wonder if building a skyscraper also builds character.

When I go to my room to find tape to hang up your paper, I pass the den. On Father's desk is a discarded drawing, with lines precise and immaculate. It is exact to a point your own lines will never be. But I turn from his plans without a glance of envy.

I know what he has lost now.

Brian

A Short Story

The Tuesday it snows I wake up early. Usually during Christmas vacation I set my clock for 10, and sometimes I don't get up even then when it rings. I like wiggling my toes under the thick quilt my grandmother made for me, enjoying the warmth and the soft feeling of the pillows behind my neck. Mostly I enjoy thinking that I am warm and snug in my own bed and that there's no school and I can sleep as long as I want. Usually "as long as I want" is 11; by then my mom is upstairs, chasing me out of bed and complaining. My mother always finds something to complain about during winter vacation. I didn't make my bed; I didn't pile up my dirty sweaters; I didn't clean up the dishes after breakfast and now she has to do the dishes plus the laundry. This Christmas, though, my mom hasn't said a word about my room or the dishes, because this Christmas my mom is busy complaining about Brian.

Remembering this makes me jump out of bed to shut off the alarm. I don't want my mother knowing that I'm up, because once she knows she'll automatically guess where I'm going. Right now, though, I'd rather concentrate on the snow piling up outside than on my mother. I reach in my closet for a sweat shirt and jeans and put them on, standing next to the window. Must be two feet of snow out there. Good. I can take him sledding.

My mom doesn't understand about Brian and me, which shouldn't surprise me because sometimes I think my mom doesn't understand me, alone, period. I remember being close to my mother when I was little. She'd sit with me on the edge of my bed when I had nightmares and she'd tuck the quilt my grandmother made for me up close to my chin. Sometimes she'd tell me stories about my grandmother, about how she made my mom hot milk with cinnamon sticks when my mom was little and had the flu. Sometimes the stories were about my mom when she was a teenager, and how she'd help my grandmother sew a new dress for a party because they couldn't afford all store-bought clothes. They'd sit in my mom's bedroom with pins on the bedspread and fabric everywhere, and while they cut out the material and sewed it together they'd talk about boys and clothes, like sisters. Once I asked my mom about what happened to my grandmother as she got old. It was hard for me to imagine the gray shadow of a person we visited in the nursing home laughing about boys. My mom never answered my question directly, just said something about everyone getting older and getting sick. My mom doesn't visit my grandmother anymore either. I still visit her, but my mom says she is better off away from us, where she can be looked after.

I think my grandmother would understand about Brian. I didn't start baby-sitting for his family until Brian was three, which was four years ago and way before anyone knew exactly what was wrong with him. Brian was my first steady baby-sitting charge and I felt pretty grown-up, holding his hand when we crossed the street and making sure we checked the traffic light. When I got the job I thought I'd be really bored spending Saturday mornings with a three-year-old, and at first some of the girls teased me about liking Brian better than boys in our class — for instance, Todd Molloy, who was a big deal back then in eighth grade. My friends and I spent hours talking about Todd and hatching plans to run into him, but whatever we planned I made sure I kept Saturday mornings free. Saturday mornings belonged to Brian.

I liked everything about Brian, I really did. I liked playing with him in the sandbox and pushing him on the swings. I liked the way he'd share his toys with me, the way only little kids share, without prompting. I liked the way he asked me questions without worrying about hurting my feelings or being polite. Brian always came out with whatever was on his mind. And I liked the way he gave me hugs and kisses all the time. Most people thought he just was fond of me especially, but Brian gave affection to everyone we met. I remember bringing him to my house once when my mom was home and he gave her a huge bear hug the minute he was in the door. My mother mentioned it to me later, after I took Brian home. "He's a friendly little boy, isn't he? But isn't he — well, a little *demonstrative* with strangers?"

I didn't mind her comments about the way Brian hugged and kissed people. But then I didn't mind most of the things that seemed to bother people about Brian. Once when he was four we were walking down the street, and Brian ran to the postman with his blue bag stuffed with mail. "Well, hi, little guy!" The postman kneeled down. "Are you looking at the mail? Can you say MAIL?" "Agaa!" Brian tried. "That's good, Bri, almost right," I told Brian. But the postman was giving Brian a critical look. "Pretty big not to talk right, isn't he?" he said to me. I grabbed Brian's hand and took him down the street fast.

It was true that Brian didn't talk very well. He didn't do most things as well as the other little kids I knew, but he tried harder and got most everything done if he did things slowly. And he thought about what he was doing, much more than other children do. I remember showing him how to pour sand into a pail with his toy shovel. It seemed easy enough to me when I picked up the shovel and scooped it down into the sandbox, but when I looked at Brian's face I saw that he was really concentrating. Sometimes I would see Brian with his mom in their backyard on Sundays, and she'd be showing him how to shovel the way I showed him on Saturday mornings. Most of the time his mom would be smiling and I'd think everything was fine, but sometimes I caught the look on her face as she watched Brian's confusion, and I'd remember the postman and my mom and what everyone said about Brian.

And people talked about Brian all the time, it seemed. I don't remember when they first started doing it, but I do remember the first time I realized what was happening. It was the Sunday after Brian's first week in kindergarten, and I was standing in the fruits and vegetables aisle at Ferguson's. Grocery shopping is my job when I don't have too much homework, because another one of my mom's complaints is that I never help around the house. "There's no reason why you can't go to the store and get what I need," she always tells me. "You eat here, too, after all, don't forget!" I never forget because she always reminds me, which is why Mr. Ferguson knows me so well and how I ended up at his store that Sunday, looking for the stuff on my mom's list. My mom likes putting her grocery list in alphabetical order, which is easier for her when she writes it down but murder for me, because I end up hitting the same aisle a dozen times. That Sunday it was N-nectarines, which landed me in fruits and vegetables, and while I was busy examining the fruit I saw Mrs. Medea and Mrs. Simson down the aisle. Mrs. Medea and Mrs. Simson live three blocks from my house; they each have two children and talk about the Sunday School play and PTA meetings. I do not usually eavesdrop on Mrs. Medea and Mrs. Simson. I wouldn't have eavesdropped that day, either, except that as I left the aisle in search of R-raisins I heard Brian's name.

I wasn't sure at first. It could have been any name sounding like his. And if they did say Brian, there are other Brians in the world, aren't there? But I stopped looking for R-raisins anyway and went back to fruits and vegetables, pretending to study the tomatoes and listening to every word I could hear. I heard too much.

"Well, now, I know I only have a mother's opinion, although after two children I should certainly *know*, but anyway Mrs. Greene is a *professional*, and she told me confidentially he's the slowest boy in her class."

"Oh, I *know*, and frankly, dear, it's really beginning to disturb me. I don't know if I want my Stephanie playing with. . . ." I was gone. Out of fruits and vegetables. Out of the grocery. Leaving behind N-nectarines and R-raisins in the shopping cart, and running as fast as I could down the block. All the time I was running I thought about Mrs. Medea and Mrs. Simson, who talked about Brian in a supermarket, and about Mrs. Greene, the kindergarten teacher, who talked about Brian outside the classroom, and I wondered if people had always been talking about Brian, all those years, in all the time before I learned to listen.

I made a point of listening after that. I sometimes wonder if Brian listened, too, if the new way he clung to me when we went to the park on Saturdays was because of the kids there, running in the sandbox and playing on the swings and looking at Brian. I thought they were just being friendly at first, looking at him and wondering if he wanted to play, but after a while I saw they were giving him a quick glance and looking away, the way you do when you're five and your mother's told you a hundred times it's not polite to stare at people who are different. I wondered what their mothers had told them exactly. I wondered if they would have liked Brian on their own. I didn't think they would have realized he was different from them, or would have cared, because I knew Brian didn't care much about what he couldn't do. I always thought Brian wouldn't have known he had problems, if only everyone didn't make such a point of pointing them out to him.

I played with Brian alone that fall, in any case. Sometimes we'd pick up stones and throw them in the little pond and sometimes we'd look for four-leaf clovers in the grass. A lot of the time we walked around looking at trees, and I'd tell Brian all their names, the way I learned them in horticulture class. Brian remembered a few of the easy names, but what he liked better was to stand still and look up past their trunks to their very top leaves. I must have spent an awful lot of time before that autumn with my nose to the sidewalk, hurrying, because I never really looked up at the treetops before, that I can remember. I figured you just had to be Brian's age to do that, but later, when I got to noticing that the other kids sped by on tricycles or ran by, looking down at the grass, I figured you just had to be Brian.

I liked it best those times alone in the park. I liked looking at trees with Brian, away from the people who liked looking at Brian himself. I taught him things — things my mom said he should already have known at his age — and he made mistakes, but when I told him he was doing fine he believed me. I thought it would stay like that, me encouraging and him believing, but I forgot about the rest of the world. The Mrs. Medeas of the world, and their children, hadn't disappeared, and they were making themselves known to Brian that fall. I remember once after we finished playing tag, a little boy who'd been watching from the sandbox came near us. I was dusting off Brian's overalls, trying to get grass stains off his wiggly body, and then retying the sneakers that came loose when he ran. I always folded Brian's fingers around his laces when I tied his shoes, moving his hands and arms with mine and hoping he'd catch on well enough to do it himself sometime soon. The little boy standing by us watched while I tied Brian's shoes with Brian's "help." "Can't he tie his own shoes? I can. I'm four!" I told him that Brian needed a little help sometimes but that he was getting better all the time. I was talking more to Brian than to the little boy, the way I always did, but this time I saw something change in Brian's face. He was too slow to tie his shoes but suddenly quick enough to know it *mattered*, and the look in his eyes made my knuckles white with anger. I wanted to shake my fists at the irony of it all. Half the kids and most of the adults in town would have said they were more intelligent than Brian, and not one of them was smart enough to pick on someone their own size.

Including my mother. My mother's been on my back about Brian for a year, bugging me about the time I spend with him when I should be doing Other Things. Other Things means going out with teenage boys, who pick you up at eight and keep you out till all hours and leave your mother hysterical because she's been waiting up for you all night. My mother is dying to wait up for me all night. I think she wants to have all the problems the other mothers have, so she can call up the neighbors and cluck her tongue over my antics. I wear too much makeup, she doesn't know who my friends are, the boy who took me to the movies has a car he drives too fast. As it is, my mother knows where I am every Saturday, so she's mad because I'm robbing her of her chance to get gray hairs. My mother has nothing to worry about, so naturally, being my mother, she worries twice as much about that.

At first her complaints were just a little annoying, because they centered on me and all the things I should be doing, and those are the complaints I've been hearing all my life.

I should be going to the library to study instead of baby-sitting; I should be going shopping with that nice Marcie Adams from down the street instead of baby-sitting; I should be cleaning up the mess in my room instead of baby-sitting. For a while I did all the things she suggested, studying hard on Friday nights and cleaning my room when I got home from school and going shopping with Marcie on Sunday mornings, but leaving Saturdays free for Brian like always. After a while, though, I realized it wasn't the studying or the shopping my mother cared about. She was just looking to fill up my Saturday mornings with anything but Brian. If there had been a Saturday morning class at the Y on poisonous snakes, my mother would have lectured me on the importance of learning all about reptiles.

I could have taken her campaign against my baby-sitting Brian and shrugged it off, but just this past winter I noticed a change in her complaints I couldn't ignore. Instead of complaining about my seeing Brian, she started complaining about Brian himself. Most of her ammunition she got from her friends who had kids in Brian's class: Did you know that your friend Brian can't say his alphabet yet? I heard Brian has a little trouble buttoning his coat before recess. Some of the ammunition I'm afraid she got from me, from the way I boasted about all the things he was learning when I came home on Saturdays. I was always so proud of Brian that I

59

mentioned it every time he counted to 10 or knew his colors, and then my mother would raise her eyebrows to remind me that most of the kids his age had been doing that stuff for years.

So I stopped talking about Brian at home. I stopped telling about how he looked at tree-tops and how I, too, was learning to look at treetops, and how he learned to tie his own shoes by himself just last month, and how we drew turkeys on construction paper to hang in his room this Thanksgiving. I stopped mentioning where we went and what we did once we got there, and maybe sometimes I wouldn't mention that we were going anywhere at all, just sneak out of the house before my mother got up on Saturday mornings.

Which is what I am doing today. I reach for the comb and give my hair a quick brush-through, tying it quickly in a ponytail I know will untie out in the snow. I reach for a sweater, making sure it has pockets, and walk quietly down the stairs to the kitchen for two snacks. I stuff apples and chocolate bars in my pockets, and then I rummage through the vegetable bin, trying to be quiet. I find one carrot there and I polish it off quickly, rubbing the dirt off and then washing my hands. The running water makes more noise than I would have liked, but that carrot will make the greatest nose for a snowman.

I turn the water off and walk down the hall to the closet, keeping my socked feet on tip-toes and trying to listen for noise. I open the closet door and reach for my boots, and I don't hear my mother until the second boot is halfway on.

She is up already, downstairs on the phone. The living room is one room and a hallway away from me, so maybe I can still get out without her hearing. I finish zipping my boot and tie on a big scarf. I walk three feet in my mom's direction and tilt my head a little. The telephone cord drags out of the living room. Good. Still talking. My gloves are somewhere deep in my pocket and when I rummage around for them my hat slides off. I put my hat on and reach to close the closet door, and when I let go of the doorknob I hear Brian's name. It doesn't hit me for a minute or two. I am so used to not talking about Brian anymore, so used to not listening when my mother mentions him and complains, that his name sounds strange coming out of my living room. I am sneaking out of my house to see a person whose name I never mention, and my mother is sitting down the hall in the living room, talking about the person I'm sneaking to see.

I should have learned my lesson by now, but I go closer to the telephone to hear her anyway. Her voice rises and falls the way it does when she's excited, and she talks quickly, like she knows all the answers to her questions anyway.

". . . think you're absolutely right mumble mumble should have done it before. No, I don't think it's interfering at all mumble it's the job of concerned parents mumble bring it to the principal's attention . . . special schools after all for children like him mumble sure the mother will agree must be a burden on her, too, no use pretending he's not retarded . . . not retarded . . . not retarded. . . ."

I grab my coat and run out the door. I think about Mrs. Medea and how I ran out of the supermarket. I think about Brian not knowing how to say the alphabet, and about Brian teaching me to look up to the sky at the trees. I think about my grandmother being sent to where people could care for her, when she got old and different, and I think about Brian and how everyone said he was not like the others. I think about Brian, learning everything slower than the others, and knowing more than the others did to begin with.

My mother hangs up the telephone when she hears the front door slam. I run down the driveway in record time, and I see her out of the corner of my eye, on the porch. I want to keep running but I remember the sled, and I backtrack quickly to the garage. I reach for the sled's handle and tug it out to the drive. A glove falls off. Let it stay where it is.

I walk down the drive and into the street toward Brian's. From halfway down the block I can still see my mother, standing out in the yard with her eyes on me. Her mouth is open and I know she's yelling, calling my name and telling me to come back. She will scream down the block that she wants to explain.

But I do not hear her. She is very far away.

4. Cystic Fibrosis

My doctor walked into my hospital room a few weeks ago, shaking his head in a mixture of amusement and frustration. "I just called in an admission," he told me, referring to a c.f. friend of mine who needed to be hospitalized. "And when I told the admissions clerk that the problem was c.f., she said, 'Oh, yes. C.f. Cerebral palsy.'"

I've had the same problem myself. I can't count how many times I've told people I have cystic fibrosis and they've asked me where my crutches were, or why I hadn't lost my hair, or where I caught my sickness. The misinformation that circulates about cystic fibrosis is so ludicrous as to be funny, except for one thing: There are hundreds of kids born every year with c.f. who don't get diagnosed for years because of misinformation and myths, because doctors as well as parents don't know the facts about cystic fibrosis, don't know what the latest treatments are or where their local c.f. center is, don't know what cystic fibrosis means, or even how to pronounce the words. I've had friends whose medical care was grossly inadequate for many years, because doctors mistook their symptoms for bronchitis, for failure to thrive, for asthma, for croup. And there is nothing funny about not getting the medical treatment your sick body depends on. There is nothing funny about children ending up in their graves because a monster goes undiagnosed.

The ironic thing, of course, is that for all the puzzled stares its name brings, cystic fibrosis is not at all uncommon. In fact, the National Cystic Fibrosis Foundation estimates that c.f. kills more kids in the U.S. than any other inherited disease — an average of three kids per day. That's more deaths caused by one sickness than by polio, rheumatic fever, and diabetes combined. What's more, the C.F. Foundation says that in the U.S. today there are at least 30,000 people still fighting cystic fibrosis, and anywhere from 1,500 to 2,200 new cases diagnosed each year. If you're starting a family, as my parents once were, and you're thinking about cribs and names and formulas, you don't dwell on statistics; but the fact is that cystic fibrosis shows up in one out of every 1,600 births. That's a lot of kids if you stop seeing the figures and start seeing the reality: That's one kid out of the student body of any large high school. That's one kid out of the population of any small town. That's one kid who could be your kid, or your friend's kid, or a cousin or a niece or a member of your town's Brownie troop. A lot of parents of newly diagnosed c.f. children have told me that they'd never heard of the disease, and they'd thought their friends hadn't, either, until they started asking around and found that their neighbors knew a 30-year-old man with c.f. and their butcher's daughter had a little boy with c.f. just starting school. It's everywhere, it really is, in the United States and in England and in Israel and in many other countries; among people who are affluent enough to pay for medical care on their own and people whose entire life savings would be wiped out by paying for one month's worth of c.f. treatment; among white people and Hispanic people and black people and, according to the C.F. Foundation, sometimes even Oriental people. People I have spoken to get c.f. mixed up with m.d. [muscular dystrophy] and c.p. [cerebral palsy] and m.s. [multiple sclerosis] and a hundred other similar-sounding illnesses, but c.f. is not uncommon enough to be so unheard-of. It is there, relentlessly out there, right this minute, and for too many kids, maybe one that you know, it is as close as breathing.

My parents took me to the doctor as a child because I wasn't gaining weight. Not entirely unusual, but then I was eating like a small horse, devouring everything in sight and looking for more. With an appetite like that, my parents expected a chubby little baby, but the food seemed to go right through me in the form of loose and smelly bowel movements. By the time I was a year old, my mom was as dismayed by the number of diaper changes I required daily as she was by my weight: 15 pounds. My pediatrician, who oddly enough later left his private practice to head the cystic fibrosis center at the hospital where I'm still treated, suspected I had c.f. and ordered the appropriate work-up. C.f. is diagnosed via a "sweat test" or procedure that measures salt content in the sweat. Since the sweat in c.f. patients has an abnormally high salt content, the diagnosis using this test is usually easy to make once the child starts producing sweat, at the age of one or two months. The test is also simple and painless and, most of the time, highly accurate. But not in my case. In my case the procedures goofed. My first sweat test showed that I most certainly did not have cystic fibrosis, much to the relief of my parents, who had not anyway understood the kindly doctor's explanation of this cystic-something-or-other.

Dr. Heffer, having no reason to doubt the test results, began a campaign to put weight on his little patient. Unfortunately, he chose the wrong approach. In cystic fibrosis the basic defect is a thick, sticky mucus that clogs up the passageways in the body. Breathing problems are caused by mucus clogging up the airways and the lungs, and digestive problems are caused when mucus stops the flow of enzymes from the pancreas into the small intestine, causing food to be poorly

66

digested. Malabsorption of food is especially common in the case of fatty foods, which are not easily digested by even the healthy person. Because he had proof positive that I did not have c.f., Dr. Heffer suggested that my mom feed me strained bacon, cereal with butter, sour cream — anything fatty enough to put the weight on. It was a horrible, though of course unintentional, error, and I baffled the doctors even more now by losing pounds instead of gaining. Finally, when I was 13 months old, the obvious could no longer be denied and a repeat sweat test was ordered. The results — we still have the paper somewhere, tucked in all the old medical records — showed cystic fibrosis. Unreally. Unbelievably. But unquestionably. I had cystic fibrosis.

My mother, having been shown once before that sweat tests were not 100-percent foolproof, demanded a third test immediately, and what did the doctors know anyway, and if I really had this cystic thing how was it none of these medical geniuses had discovered it earlier? The third test was also positive. That week the doctors discharged a little girl from the hospital, a girl who most certainly had this cystic-whatever-you-call-it, who also now had two confused parents and a need for medications and treatments those parents could not begin to pronounce. I was bright, I was happy, and I was, not incidentally, two pounds heavier, thanks to the new low fat diet and the medications all c.f. kids are placed on. But, of course, to my parents' eyes, I was forever altered. A year earlier, they had brought home from the hospital a newborn who surely had the whole world at her fingertips. Now they were coming home, again from the hospital, with a 13-month-old who was incurably ill. Who would need treatments every day of every year just to stay on an even keel. Who would need worse treatments if ever her disease got worse. Who would, according to the pamphlets available on c.f. in 1965, die before she was 11. Before she went to the prom. Before she had a Sweet 16 party. Before she made her parents grandparents. My parents loved me all the same, but they never again looked at me in quite the same way, with the same ease of mind. You can tell. You can see it in my baby photos, before I was diagnosed and after. People say that c.f. is a progressive disease, getting worse over time, and of course they're right. But you can look at the eyes of a parent being told his kid has cystic and watch them change in a minute. It happens. I think people change forever in that minute.

My own parents' eyes were probably more filled with confusion than fear. They went home from the hospital not only with their daughter but with an instruction sheet baffling enough to confound Dr. Spock. Some of the treatments were easy to understand; the orders to keep me away from greasy foods, the pill called Cotazym, which would help me digest the food my own body couldn't handle.

Some of the treatments, designed to prevent lung damage, were more complicated. I needed to sleep in a mist tent, a canopylike structure that blows cool, damp air on the patient so she breathes easier. I needed to use an aerosol mask, a small oxygen-type mask filled with medications I could breathe in to thin out my mucus. I needed to have a horribly primitive treatment called postural drainage, which involves clapping on the ribs of the c.f. child so that the mucus loosens and she can cough it up. I needed to avoid diving into swimming pools at all costs, in order to avoid putting extra pressure on my lungs. I needed, it must have seemed to my mother, a full-fledged Supernurse, someone much more skilled than this nervous new mother who only one month ago had been mainly concerned with whether or not her daughter was too young for a tricycle. Now she had questions scary enough to warrant two or three calls to Dr. Heffer every day: How much medicine goes in the aerosol mask? What if Robyn doesn't like the mist tent? How much Cotazym should we give Robyn before a glass of skim milk? Before a cheese sandwich and Twinkies?

I don't remember much from those first scary days, but I do remember certain people who made my frightened parents less frightened. One of my earliest memories is of my mist tent breaking down, and my mother making frantic calls to have someone fix the machine she was sure my every breath depended on. The hero in this story is named

Milton, and he came very often after that to fix my mist tent, because, as he told my mother, he had two strong hands and a granddaughter of his own with cystic fibrosis.

Things got better, as things do, when my parents gained confidence. They knew how much Cotazym I needed before all the junk food every preschooler craves. They learned to make the plastic covering for my mist tent on their own. My mother learned to give me postural drainage on the dining room table, the only place high enough for her to get the leverage she needed to pound out the mucus. We fell into the pattern of thinking that all would be all right, that the disease would always be just a little inconvenience. My mother remembers actually complaining to someone once that her five-year-old was so terribly burdened because she couldn't eat chocolate ice cream at all. Kids were dying with cystic fibrosis, kids my mom knew through the local C.F. Foundation, but they were very sick all their lives, and I had a mild case. We said it like a chant in those days — mild case, mild case, as if to ward off evil spirits. Today when I hear c.f. parents saying the same words I feel sad for them. The mildest case of cystic fibrosis progresses sometime. Mild cases mean you appreciate every day your kid is healthier than he might have been. Mild cases mean you're safe for now, but not for always, because there's no such thing as just slightly progressive. There's no such thing as just slightly fatal.

I had a "mild case" of cystic fibrosis until I was 16, and then the bottom dropped out and I was hospitalized again and again. Not too often at first — maybe three or four times that first year. But then the lung infections started coming more often, and the pills I was given started working less and less effectively. The most frustrating horror of cystic fibrosis might well be pseudomonas, a nagging lung infection that builds up in the thick mucous of c.f. patients. Once it's there, it's terribly difficult to get rid of, especially using the oral antibiotics that might allow the c.f. patient to stay at home. There was a time when I had regular bouts with pseudomonas, which were fought and won by the pills Dr. Doyle prescribed, leaving no trace of the infection. Now the pseudomonas is there all the time, like the enemy, turning my mucus green and thick and ugly. I go into the hospital every six weeks or so, to fight the miserable stuff with 10 to 14 days' worth of intravenous medicines. I used to need needles inserted in my veins for this procedure, but as I grew older my veins grew harder and harder to enter. To solve matters, I had a wonderful device inserted in my chest wall called an Infusaport catheter, which is completely unnoticeable and which allows my doctors to give me whatever IV antibiotics I need, for the price of only one needle stick. And all this is to say that, with any luck at all, my hospital stays are pretty painless and routine these days — if you can call it routine to be in a hospital for over 150 days a year, away from the home and the school where your healthy mind thrives but your sick lungs flounder.

Sometimes, when I walk the halls of my hospital late at night, I think about those lungs, and about all that c.f. has done for me, and to me, through the years. Things have changed since I was first diagnosed with c.f. Kids with c.f. don't take Cotazym anymore. They take Pancrease. Kids with c.f. don't sleep in mist tents anymore. Doctors think the plastic breeds pseudomonas. And kids with c.f. don't have a 50-50 shot of living to be 11 anymore. The median age of survival went up to 21. Those facts show progress, but of course, if you're living with c.f., progress isn't good enough. You get impatient. You want cures yesterday. You want to wake up tomorrow with your lung scars gone and your dead friends healthy.

The piece that follows probably applies to any chronic illness, any disability that doesn't outwardly show but nevertheless changes what you do and who you are. Hidden disabilities are hard to describe and even harder to relate to, but maybe this one terrifying fact will bring it home: Cystic fibrosis is an inherited illness. To get it, you must be born with one c.f. gene from your mother and one from your father, but there is absolutely no way of finding out who carries the c.f. gene. So scientists don't know which of us have the potential to give c.f. to our kids, but they know this: There are 30 million carriers of cystic fibrosis walking around out there. That's one out of every 20 Americans with the potential to pass on a genetic killer. And so the next time you're thinking about hidden handicaps, about hidden time bombs, remember this: One out of every 20 people you meet on the street may someday fall in love, may someday marry and make plans for the future with the one they love, and, unless a cure for cystic fibrosis shows up soon, may someday walk out of a hospital the way my parents did 20 years ago, with a baby, a teddy bear — and an instruction sheet telling how to do postural drainage.

Cystic Fibrosis: The Hidden Handicap

It happened the Friday before my history exam. I was rereading assignments in my college's library and needed a book located on the third floor. Seeing that the student elevator was broken, I asked the guard outside for permission to use the staff elevator. He told me he couldn't give me permission without a special reason, and I explained that I had a handicap and couldn't manage the stairs that day. Staring at my two strong legs, he became suspicious. "Are you making this up?" he asked. "You don't look handicapped."

It's true. I don't. Unlike the majority of students registered with my school's Office for Disabled Students, I am not visibly impaired in any way. I do not require crutches, a wheelchair, a guide dog, or any aid that might alert people to my condition. Yet when faced with six flights of stairs to climb, or a five-minute interval between classes seven blocks apart, I am as limited as my friends who need braces or a walker. It is a fact that one does not *see* my problems until I am challenged beyond my capabilities, but my problems are with me all the time nevertheless. I was born with what can be termed a "hidden handicap" — cystic fibrosis.

Doctors define cystic fibrosis as a chronic obstructive lung and digestive disease. Simply put, this means that I was born with abnormally thick mucus which clogs, instead of lubricates, the passages to my lungs and digestive system. The presence of this mucus in two different systems of my body leads to two different sets of problems for me. Because mucus blocks the passages to my digestive organs, I have trouble digesting food, especially fatty or greasy foods like chocolate and potato chips. A pill called Pancrease, which aids in digestion, allows me to eat almost anything, but I am still on a low fat, high calorie diet, and have trouble gaining weight.

My more serious problems, though, are caused by mucus blocking the air passages to my lungs. This leads to many respiratory difficulties, including frequent hospitalizations, shortness of breath, and a productive cough that never goes away. In the past, c.f. victims have died before reaching school age, but new medicines combating infections now enable c.f. kids to live well into adulthood. Although I am grateful to have potential that past victims of this disease only dreamt of, being a teen with c.f. is not easy. Since c.f. progresses as the patient gets older, the number of my infections and hospitalizations has increased, and the amount of activity I can endure easily has decreased, since I turned 16 three years ago. In short, my problem is that I am a "handicapped" teenager whose handicaps aren't fixed but have changed with time.

Not that cystic fibrosis is disabling to me every moment. On days when I am clear of mucus, I can bike-ride, run around campus, take my dogs for a walk, and keep up with my friends. Nobody notices my disease unless I have a coughing spell, which can be explained to strangers easily ("I have asthma"), and is accepted matter-of-factly by my friends who know what's behind the cough. If people ask why I'm skipping chocolate cake for dessert, I either say that I'm allergic or that I have digestive problems and they let it go. Almost all of my friends take vitamins or pills for allergies, so my pill-taking is pretty much ignored. Postural drainage, a type of therapy that keeps me decongested, is done before class and at bedtime, so no excuses have to be made to casual acquaintances who wonder where I disappear to. On days like this, the term "hidden handicap" is especially relevant — my disease is present but it doesn't disable me in the slightest.

On other days, c.f. is a more difficult handicap. Because I am prone to lung infections, I am hospitalized approximately eight times a year, for ten days to two weeks, and recently these hospitalizations have come frustratingly close together. In addition, for about three or four days before a hospitalization, I am busy doing extra therapy and taking more pills because I feel ill and want to try fighting the infection alone before going to the hospital. At all of these times I am handicapped by cystic fibrosis socially, academically, and physically.

The physical handicaps are caused by the lung infection itself. Anyone who has had asthma, bronchitis, or a chest cold can tell you that the last thing she felt like doing was climbing stairs or walking to classes or studying. When I am sick, my chest hurts from coughing and I am very tired because my body is fighting an infection. The guard at the library that day examined my legs and found them sturdy, but he had no way of knowing that there was so much mucus rattling in my chest.

Socially, c.f. has been a trial more than once. Several weeks before my first year at Barnard College began, a beloved physician who had taken care of me since I was an infant and whom I adored, died. Just weeks later my treasured friend Juliann died of c.f. It is terribly difficult to lose two people you love within a short time; harder still to watch a friend die knowing you have the same disease that killed her. I was not, to say the least, in the best of spirits during the first week of college — and my quiet, withdrawn behavior probably lost me friends when I needed them most. Indeed, months later, one of the girls from my dorm brought up this very subject. "I wanted to be friends with you way back at orientation," she said. "But you were so quiet I figured you were just not very friendly."

That was not the only instance when c.f. alienated me from other people. It is very difficult for me to make strong friendships at school because I am so frequently hospitalized. When I am sick I miss the late night pizza parties, the early morning gossip, the day-to-day sharing that builds friendships. Just as I have trouble catching up on my French after being sick, I have trouble, too, catching up on the lives of people I care about. Because of this, a lot of my best friends are kids from the hospital, who are either chronically ill like me or have diseases such as leukemia. Unfortunately, the very thing that I share with these kids — sickness — frequently dictates that I lose one of them to death. Because some of the friends I've loved most have died, I place a greater value, I think, on friendships than most 19-year-olds do.

C.f. as an educational handicap is a problem I have only grappled with recently, as my hospitalizations increase. Cystic fibrosis does *not* in any way disable a person's mental capacity, but frequent and prolonged absences often make it impossible for c.f. patients to do well in school. One of my closest friends with c.f. was a wonderful conversationalist and obviously very bright, but at 16 he was still in eighth grade, unable to catch up on the work he missed while sick. I make the distinction then very clearly: C.f. is not an intellectual handicap, but it certainly is an educational handicap.

I am currently enrolled at Barnard College in New York and am proud of the fact that although I missed much work in high school, my grades were high enough to gain me admission to some of the country's best universities. My grades at Barnard have also been good so far, and again, I am very proud. I was hospitalized over half a dozen times during my freshman year. Catching up on work often left me in despair; I was positive more than once that I'd never get through all that extra reading. My high grades, though, are partly attributable to my friends and my professors. I have had professors accept papers from me a month late without a single word of reproach; I've had other professors give me delayed exams, tape lectures for me, and assign me tutors. I had a French professor who called me in the hospital every time I was admitted: She had no make-up work for me, but wanted to know how I was feeling. An English professor I have enormous respect for let me hand in a paper *three weeks after school ended*, then told me on the phone that everyone was "really rooting for you, Robyn." And likewise, I have friends who've volunteered to tutor me in different subjects; others have copied school notes, brought me lunch while I frantically caught up on homework, etc.

Other individuals, unfortunately, have worsened my educational problems — especially professors. One high school teacher lowered my grade despite the fact that my work was as good as any of her students'; when I appealed to a chairman, he told me I was lucky: Had *he* been the teacher, I would have failed. A college professor evidently thought c.f. was an excuse to get special privileges; he told me he didn't give delayed exams to anyone for fear "of starting a trend." Coping with attitudes like these while fighting a lung infection drives me wild! Were it not for friends who rally to my side ("I think the teacher's sicker than you'll ever be, Rob"), I would not do well in school at all.

Social, academic, physical — when all areas are totaled up, am I or am I not disabled? Is a hidden handicap a genuine handicap? For the most part I am inclined to think of c.f. as a handicap, a disability. Activities are limited because of c.f. Life spans are shortened because of c.f. Huffing and puffing after walking 10 blocks, I have trouble seeing c.f. as anything less than a handicap.

But I don't always see it this way. I remember a school night last winter when I was in my room chatting with my friend

Jackie, and she happened to pick up a Rexo-graphed page of notes from my psychology class. When Jackie complained that she hated copying notes because the library copier cost so much, I told her that the Office for Disabled Students let me copy for free the notes I missed when I was sick. Getting a mischievous look on her face, Jackie teased, "Oh you, you're not disabled at all. You just want to use the copier for nothing!" We both burst out laughing, and I threw a Rexo at her. And I felt less disabled than I'd ever felt in my life.

5. Friends

When I was 16, my friend Kenny made a statement that I have never quite forgotten. We were spending a fair bit of time together, both of us stuck in the hospital nearly all winter with the pneumonia that strikes cystic kids particularly fiercely in colder months. I had begun to think I was suffering more from loneliness than from lung disease, and in one of my more self-pitying moments I pointed out to Kenny that at least he had brothers and sisters to cheer him up by phone. On and on I pathetically went, crying out that if I had to deal with sickness all the time, the least I could use was a sibling or two to help me through the rough spots. Other cystics lived in a whole house full of kids, and here I was entirely on my own. Kenny waited until I was through before disagreeing: "You've got friends. Haven't you forgotten your friends?" he said.

"Sure I have friends, Kenny. But when the going gets tough, I bet they'll split. Why should they cope? We're not family. They don't even live at my house."

He looked at me long and hard. "Better for you. They live in your heart."

He was right. In the 21 years I've lived with cystic fibrosis, and in the five years I have lived since my disease has begun progressing, I have been given nearly every medicine known to have a shot at combating lung infection, and sometimes I still think that friendship is the best antibiotic. This is not to sound melodramatic; this is to state a fact that I understand intuitively and could never outright prove: I stay out of the hospital longer when I have movie dates, concerts, sleepovers with friends in the offing. I feel better in the hospital, with or without antibiotics, when the phone is always ringing. My lungs work harder for me when my friends work for me, too.

Some of this is pretty easy to explain; I am bound to feel healthier when a whole host of friends volunteer to do my therapy, to help me set up an aerosol treatment, to buy me food from the store and so save me an extra tiring walk when I'm sick. But some things are harder to reconcile with logic; the times I've gasped for breath sitting alone in my room but miraculously felt more energetic the second a friend came to visit; the way I run out of air faster on the way home from a friend's house than on the way there; the times I could not get through giving my medical history to a nurse without choking terribly, but five minutes later could greet a room full of c.f. friends without a single cough. Doctors may disbelieve all they wish, but every bout with pneumonia that I fight through proves Kenny right — the deadly bacteria in my lungs meet their worst enemy in the living, breathing friendships I keep in my heart.

This is not to say that c.f. doesn't strain a friendship, or doesn't wreak havoc with my ability to meet new friends. When c.f. throws all of that mucus into my air passages, it throws me into the hospital as well, and into a world where people are often too sick or too scared to look for companions. And, of course, stuck in those four hospital walls as I am, all normal existence becomes more wishful thinking than everyday fact, forcing me, more times than I can count, to miss the sleepover, the pizza party, the last-minute trip to Häagen-Dazs. With all this, I should, as I told Kenny, be entirely on my own, with my social life falling victim to c.f. as quickly as my lung capacity. And certainly sometimes this seems the case, as when I quarreled only weeks ago with a friend who wanted to set up a definite date to see me, a friend who could not understand that on any given day I might be congested or even hospitalized — that you do not make definite plans with a variable disease. Then, too, I have been known to feel isolated and alone, when the flow of visitors and get well cards and good wishes tapers off from people who think of my hospitalizations as "old hat," who don't know or don't remember that even a girl who has been in the hospital so many times that she could probably write her own medical orders enjoys getting a silly note now and then. I suppose now that I'm older and well adjusted to sickness, people assume that I don't need an entire support system, and perhaps they're right. But what people forget is that age and good adjustment have very little to do with happiness, or with hope for a good future, or even with finding a reason to get up every morning and do another hour of therapy. Luckily, some friends of mine know all this by instinct, and when I remember all the bouts with pneumonia I've licked, I'd like to think I got by on a little intravenous and a lot of love.

I do not write stories about all of my friends; they are too many. But I do not forget. I do not forget how my friend Mindy once dropped all that she was doing to drag me and my books back from class on a morning when I could hardly breathe. I do not forget how my friend Elizabeth, no stranger to health problems herself, tutored me all year in a college English class, hour after hour when she could have been relaxing, and then refused all offers of payment from my school's Office for Disabled Students. I do not forget how my friend Jennifer takes all complications of c.f. matter-of-factly, convincing me the way no pep talk could that I am not weird or different or a person to shy away from, *making me laugh when I am turning blue from lack of oxygen by inquiring as to exactly what shade of blue I am becoming. ("You can be a Smurf!") I do not forget the people who work too hard and stay too busy to call me but who call anyway: Michael, Catherine, Susan. And most especially, I do not forget the nurses who were my friends when I lost a friend to cystic: Judi, Lori, Arlene, Cavaille.*

Still, some friends are too good to keep to my memories. And so more and more often I try to capture them in words, transferring all that spirit onto stiff sheets of paper. Sometimes it doesn't work; I still look back at pieces and think I could have better described his love of bad jokes, her devotion to animals, his strong fight against cancer. Sometimes I refuse to try, believing with all my heart that I cannot do justice to a few magical people. But sometimes — maybe more by luck than by skill — I come away from the typewriter with a jumble of papers true to my friends, which gives all the world just the slightest clue as to who these people are and how great my fortune runs in knowing them.

The stories that follow are my best attempts at reducing flesh and blood to pen and paper. The first piece revolves around a fact I take pride in — that not all of my friends share my age and sex and way of life. So many teenagers I know believe in the generation gap, but c.f. has taught me to like the elderly as well as the very young, to find pleasure in being with teachers many years my elder and with the little monsters who run wild through c.f. clinic, so many years my junior. When I address the Barnum cast, I address a group of extremely talented actors and actresses who kindly "adopted" me during the years their show Barnum ran on Broadway. Some of them are long gone from my life, but some of them, scattered and busy and older than I though they assuredly are, remain close friends. When Barnum closed, I wanted to pay the cast back with some sort of present, but instead I ended up thanking them for all their gifts to me. And in addition to listing all those wonderful shows of affection, I think I captured something of the love that has backed me up all these years when my own imperfect strength could not support me.

The next two pieces are about friends who shared a major aspect of my life — cystic fibrosis. Juliann and I met at c.f. clinic, on a noisy day when I was most impressed with her quiet manner and her sparkling eyes. She was younger than I by a good five years, but I never stopped feeling like a kid in the face of all her maturity. She was as capable of giggling as the next teenage girl (more capable, if she was playing gleefully with her hamster), yet something in the way she handled herself, handled her sickness, belied her few years. She did not live to see womanhood — she died before she turned 13. But I intended "Taking Leave" to capture not only my sense of fleeting time during Juliann's last few months, but also my sense that I was growing old in her presence, that her competence in dealing with c.f. "her way" taught me things about the human spirit that many people much older than I never learn. In this way at least she was a woman: She nurtured me into becoming something more.

And finally, there follows a sampling of entries from my favorite diary. During my very first hospitalization I met a boy named Danny who became a major part of my life, partly because we spent so much time together in the hospital and partly because he was a pure delight to know. My early memories of Danny remain inside my head, because when we first met I did not yet keep a diary and so did not record all his antics. But during the last year of his life, when I realized full well that c.f. was about to win a battle with this boy, I kept a diary exclusively devoted to Danny and our friendship, writing down anything uniquely and wonderfully Danny that I would not want to lose when I lost him. Some of the entries were funny: the time he started an IV on my stuffed frog. Some of the entries were sadder: the skin-and-bones look of him as c.f. took his life. And some of the entries I treasure: the time he offered to replace my lost stuffed animal with all his coveted Christmas money. None of the entries capture Danny for all he was worth, but I found something of his spirit in the ones I chose to print. Perhaps Danny's greatest attribute was his ability to understand all that I've *written here about friendship and its healing powers. To this day I wear the necklace Danny bought me years ago, on a trip to a street fair that I couldn't share because I was back in the hospital with fever. It is imitation gold, pretty but inexpensive, with small blue hearts. And I treasure it not for all the allowance he spent on it but for the speech that came with it. When I protested that he could have spent his money on the toy robot he'd been longing for, he stopped me quickly if shyly. "This," he said, fingering my new necklace, "is what friends are for."*

An Open Letter to the Barnum Cast

Dear Everyone I Love,

My dictionary defines *knowledge* as "an understanding gained by experience; a range of information; something learned and kept in the mind." As a student, I have a desk cluttered with the materials of knowledge, with the knowledge of math and science and history and French. I am told to study these books, and pass a test, and if I do, I am handed a diploma and congratulated on my knowledge.

But there are some forms of knowledge that are not taught at my school. There is the learning you gain from the places and people you spend after-school hours with, the learning that comes from watching a group of professionals do their job well. For the past two years I've spent my Saturdays at *Barnum*, and during that time I've learned more than I could ever learn in school.

Not that I have become proficient in any branch of theater. I have learned about lighting, but not enough to teach it to a friend, and I have learned about scenery, but I couldn't design a set. What I *have* learned expertly, what I have gained full knowledge of, is that friendship and love and caring and all those intangibles aren't as rare as one thinks. At *Barnum* I have learned a great many things, but mostly I have learned a great deal about the human heart.

I have learned this because of your reactions to me and to my illness. Since *Barnum* opened I have been hospitalized at least a dozen times; I have developed asthma and have had many days when being sick gets me down. There are good days, when I can run up the stairs to Michael's dressing room, and bad days, when those stairs require more than a little energy. Having a friend with health problems takes a fair bit of adjusting, and you are certainly busy and have better things to cope with. There is absolutely no reason for any of you to deal with my c.f.

But you *have* coped. You've come through for me. Not a hospitalization has gone by when I haven't received a phone call from Michael or a funny get well card from Catherine or a gift or a smile. When I am depressed about spending another week at the hospital,

I can call Navarre to hear a silly joke, or Fred to talk about my stuffed bear, or Michael to hear how the matinee went. You cannot imagine what it is like to giggle with one of you about inconsequential matters unless you've spent a week hearing about lung X rays and intravenous lines. You can't imagine what it felt like to be flooded with Christmas gifts from the cast until you've spent the holiday season in a pediatrics ward. And you can't know what you did for me when you gave me a surprise party last March 27th, unless you've ever spent the day you turned 18 in a hospital.

In all of these acts you have given me a medicine my doctors cannot — the medicine of optimism and hope, along with some of the best Saturdays of my life. You have given me countless days of being delighted by your talent, a few dozen letters filled with good wishes, and the knowledge that there is sunshine on the other side of tears. And so because of these gifts, long after the curtain at *Barnum* closes forever, there will be someone very thankful for all you've done, someone who has a better definition of friendship because you have been her friends. I wish everyone had friends like you. You are the MOST WONDERFUL people in the entire world.

My best for the future goes with you all.

Love,
Robyn S. Miller

Taking Leave

"Juliann! If you don't get a move on doing this therapy, we'll never get to the movies this afternoon. I don't know why you're so irresponsible; I do twice your therapy and I'm always on time!"

"I don't care about *you*! It's my life and it's my therapy, and I'll do what I want, so just lay off...."

Oh, Juli. Please don't let me make you angry. Only a few more months together and we're at it again, spending our time arguing and creating bad memories. And it's not that I don't try to understand what you're going through; it's just that I'm sick, but you're sicker, and I haven't learned to let you go.

You know. You understand. But lately you are exasperated at my every demand, as if every touch of mine would draw you farther into a world you must leave. It's almost as bad as all the weeks you spent taking allergy tests, when you were told it would be best if you gave up chocolate, cold turkey. You never touched a candy bar after those doctor visits, but at times you still walk with me, a little too slowly, past sweet shoppes. And now you have given up riding your bike; you avoid, even alienate, the people you were close to. If it was hard for the little girl that you were to give up chocolate, how much harder is it now, at 11, to give up life?

Not that you give up completely — not you! I walk with you in the park when I take the dogs out, giving you the slower dog's leash so you will not tire. Still you manage to run wildly through the grass, my spaniel barking as you chase him through the fields. You enjoy the abandon of running so much — what it means to have legs, to have the energy to be free! I never have the heart to stop your play before you cough, and then I curse helplessly in my mind, that you cannot run without pain.

It is something you don't deal with, this feeling of helplessness. Dying is a force you can fight against with your best shot, but watching someone die is a passive thing to do. I can tell you to take your medication and do your therapy, but what to do when the medication and the therapy do not heal? If I go into a forest and scream my rage among the trees, will my hysteria help you or will my throat become sore?

Still, it is your feelings I fight more than my own. This summer, your learning to deal with the past as forever past, has perhaps been your way of accepting the absence of a future. You do not open yourself as you once did to me, curling up at a sleepover and telling me your deepest secrets. Once I could make you cry with a glance; now you are somewhere in a cocoon by yourself. You would try, I believe, to draw as far away as possible, because you want no ties to anyone of this world. And it is hard because my way of dealing with loss is the opposite — I would have you every second, for my friend, while we have time. I know that caring for me as you do, you must leave me now, even before you go, but that does not stop a part of me from wishing you could stay.

And so these days, as opposites, we are arguing more and forgiving less. And we spend time fighting a disease in different ways, but together; and we grow, but apart, as you start to take leave.

It is not fair, this gradual leave-taking of a child. If it were fair it would not be being fought by so many doctors, working with science to accomplish what you and I need so much. And if I wait eagerly to see a medical miracle, how can I make you understand I have longed for it to come in time to save *you*?

You will not be here then, when they cure your disease. You will long since have taken your leave. But you will be a party to the victory, nonetheless, on that day, and then our fight will be over, and something of the world will be at peace.

Juliann died of cystic fibrosis on August 28, 1982, two months short of her thirteenth birthday.

The Days of His Life: Danny

You're a born charmer, and I'll bet you know it. Today you jump up and down, practically dance all around me, begging me to go down to the cafeteria to buy you a Coke. You will give me the money for it, you tell me solemnly, and I'll even get a tip. But you are counting on me to understand that you simply can't do this act for yourself because, if you leave your TV now, you'll miss the best part of the monster movie. I start to laugh at your 13-year-old logic, but you remain serious; you *need* this soda. If you don't have it, you might die of thirst right in the middle of *Godzilla Meets the Two-Headed Creature*. This is obviously a very serious problem, I tell you through giggles, and I also compliment you on your fine choice of educational programs. *Godzilla* will do much to improve your mind. But you ignore my half-hearted protests, cajoling and grinning, thrusting quarters in my hands and urging me to hurry. Every part of your face not covered by smile is covered by freckles. "Stop using those freckles to manipulate me!" I tell you sternly, but I am already halfway to the cafeteria when I say it.

Daily, I see less of you and more of the disease. Your freckles are disappearing into your bony face, and no matter what rock T-shirt you have on, your barrel chest protrudes. You are really, really skinny. And the cough that I think of as under my control when it strikes me, seems to attack you all the time and knock you off your feet in its power. You cough convulsively when you laugh, which is all the time. Your face turns beet red and I can see the muscles on your forehead twitch as you choke and grab for tissues. I try to be nonchalant, bringing you paper towels (doubled, the way you like them) and telling you calmly, "Cough it *up*, Danny." I did these same things when you were 11. But there is a radical difference here: Never has your cough had so much power, as if it were a force all of its own. Telling you to "cough it up" is senseless. You gasp out, "Won't come up," and keep trying to get air. There is nothing casual about this scene, no matter how hard I try for matter-of-factness; nothing casual or calm about the panic in my heart, either. Looking at you, I sometimes feel I can *see* cystic fibrosis, as a *being*, and I am frightened for us both.

We are a lot alike, and it still surprises me. I used to think that good friends needed to be the same age, the same sex, live in the same neighborhood. I was wrong. I have lots of girl friends from high school who call me to talk about records and boys and homework, but none of them shares with me my love for stuffed animals as you do; none of them religiously watches *The Honeymooners* and likes jigsaw puzzles and does hook rugs. You and I have all these things in common plus more, and when I sit with you choosing names for your new stuffed gorilla, I still can't believe my luck in finding someone so much like me. Tonight I drag my IV pole into your room at 11:30, and we laugh as Ralph Kramden tells Alice to go to the moon. Other people, nurses and patients, wander in and out as we're watching, but they must not feel the same sense of sharing we have together. You have in common with Tommy girls and rock concerts and drinking beer and all the other things brothers stick together on; you have in common with Mike and Keith an occasionally dirty grin and a whole host of filthy jokes; but some things belong to me and you only, and it still surprises and pleases me that I can have so much fun with a boy five years my junior. You've opened my eyes to a lot of things, and perhaps one of the most significant is that, c.f. aside, I'm a really lucky girl.

You hate oxygen. You hate the mask because it stops you from talking. You hate the nasal cannula because it "makes my nose itch." You hate everything about oxygen, and maybe you hate most your growing need for it. In any case, it is always ordered for your room, and we have to fight tooth and nail to get you to use it for more than five minutes. Is it because I know you hate it, because I know you'll never put it on unless you *really* need it, that I go to pieces inside these days when I enter your room and there you are, sleeping with oxygen? No one has made you put it on. No one could. It is your own decision, your own once-very-rare-but-now-frequent concession to cystic fibrosis. If Dr. Doyle walks in, you tell her a nurse told you to put the mask on. If your brother walks in, you tell him Dr. Doyle said it would help your headaches. But the truth is that you — the c.f. kid least likely to complain or to even slightly suggest that you need help — you have decided that you need oxygen, and you are wearing the mask more and more often when I come in. If it were Michael, if it were me or Keith, I would say, "Well, everyone needs oxygen every so often and it makes sense to use it." But because it is you, I shudder every time I see it. A not-quite-five-foot-tall skinny boy with freckles and a masked face, a boy I've grown to love, and getting worse all the time.

We are exchanging Christmas presents early this year. Right now, in early December, we are both stuck in the hospital, but c.f. varies so much daily that we cannot both count on being here in two weeks. So I ask you what you want best, and you give me a list that makes me laugh: a hodgepodge of things that reflect your growing interest in girls and dating, and some gifts that you treasured at 11 and apparently haven't outgrown. You need, you tell me in the same breath, both cologne and a new stuffed bear. The cologne is the key ticket to making the girls in high school fall at your feet; everyone likes a sexy-smelling boy, isn't that right?

Cologne will make you smell great. I stifle a desire to point out that changing your socks once in a while will have the same effect, and put cologne on top of my shopping list for you. You also wouldn't mind a jar of your favorite food, pickles. Even considering the dietary restrictions of cystic fibrosis, I kid, you eat the strangest meals I have ever encountered. I know your mom well enough to believe she serves you three good meals a day, but once at the hospital you live happily in a world of Mountain Dew sodas, caramels, and, of course, pickles. There is no way I am buying anyone a jar of pickles for Christmas. Are you listening to me, Danny? Yes, he hears me, but I did ask him what he wanted best. Well, then, he has a choice between the pickles and the cologne. Almost grown-up, but not quite, he opts for the pickles. I wrap up a jar of sweet and sours and a stuffed Odie dog, feeling like a damned fool but laughing all the time. When I tell Dr. Sergiou what I bought Danny for Christmas, he warns me to enjoy it while I can: Next year he may request a Cadillac, to go, of course, with his pickles.

You are not who you were, and it shows up in countless ways. Today I visit you in the room you share with Keith: The two of you watch cartoons and you carefully fill me in on the plot of *Popeye*. You want a Coke, a hamburger, and my undivided attention as you tell me all the goriest parts of the movie

Gremlins. You are the Danny I love, but it's a horribly temporary state: The cough hits and you disappear, and everywhere there is cystic fibrosis. When you emerge you are not the same, asking only for Tylenol and oxygen, and I curse at any illness that can turn my freckle-faced livewire into a victim. Fifteen-year-old boys should live up to all their possibilities. Fifteen-year-old boys should not need oxygen while they're watching *Popeye.* Fifteen-year-old boys should sprout and grow and become always more, and here is my favorite not-quite-15-year-old doing little and becoming less. I like you just the way you are, cough and boniness and all, but something inside me will always remember all you were before the disease destroyed you — will always wonder about all the Dannys that c.f. never let you become.

I always say I believe in Heaven. I believe the books I've read about life after death, about a warm light greeting the spirit and about being peaceful and happy in eternal life. I believe you leave the dead body — a diseased, broken body — behind forever when you die. I repeat this often to the other kids. "No one is sick in Heaven," I tell Danny. "No cancer, no cystic, no anything." He believes me, and I believe it, too. But sometimes I wonder if I'm not believing in what I say out of necessity, out of self-defense. It is nice to know with assurance that I will be rid of cystic when I die. It is nice — more than nice, enormously comforting — to know that Danny will be out of his pain. But am I believing in these things simply because it *is* a comfort to do so, because I *need* to believe? They say there are no atheists in battlefield foxholes, and perhaps there are no disbelievers in God's mercy among cystics. I want so badly not to have cystic that I suspect, mostly at night or when I'm having a "down" day, that I have entirely fabricated this Heaven-without-disease, invented it because I would give anything so gladly to make it true.

I hurt for you, but I'm on the sidelines. Today I watch you from a chair near your bed, your chest strangely still and your stomach pumping madly. You cannot get air, and I cannot give you any. C.f. has thrown me all kinds of pain but nothing equals this: watching my friend slowly dying, hurting horribly for someone who is hurting even more. When you are free of pain you are animated, social; but when the headaches and the cough start you are entirely on your own, not quite 15 but struggling with forces I have never encountered and cannot help you fight. I see it clearly now as a boxing match, Danny vs. Cystic Fibrosis, and I watch you from the audience taking blow after blow and getting beaten. I want to scream at the Referee I believe in to fix this match and make you win, but I am reduced to tears every night when I say fervent prayers on your behalf. I have never pleaded like this for anything in my life, but I'm pleading now: I want my friend to live. All else is meaningless. Just let him stay alive.

Sometimes it happens this way: Your whole universe changes and you do not know of it for hours. The world as you knew it falls to pieces, never to be the same again, and you go on thinking that things are as always because you do not know better yet. Three days ago, I baby-sat for Matthew all morning, ate a few meals, liked the warm sun, saw a movie. The world was comforting, the way I knew it. And when I came home from the movie I found out it was all a farce, that the world had changed hours ago but I wasn't told until now. Robyn Blander, the nurse from the hospital, called my mother: Danny is dead.

Danny is dead.

He dies at 8:35 Saturday morning, after a horrible night of hallucinations and futile gasps for breath, or so I'm told. His mother is with him; the nurses ask her to leave as Danny stops breathing and his heart beats on. It only takes several minutes. Dr. Doyle comes at 8:45 to disconnect the heart monitor, all business, the nurses say, until she walks away from Danny's bed, and then she cries. I have never seen her cry, can't imagine it, but then I am also having trouble imagining Danny dead, and a universe without him.

My mom gets the call from Robyn that evening. They've lost my phone number upstate, they have been trying for days to warn me. I would have come home. I would have rushed home, but now it is too late to see Danny off, to kiss him good-bye. I can touch memories, but how meager compared to touching the boy, compared to laughing with, yelling at, talking to Danny.

My mother tells me she has bad news a few minutes after I come home from the movie. My mouth stops in midsentence, I-know-I-know, but I cannot say it. Instead I take wild stabs. "Aunt Ida's dead?" I guess — badly. Aunt Ida is too healthy to die, and her death would never put this grayness on my mother's face. "Danny," I say. My mother is crying and nodding. "No . . ." I tell her fiercely. Is there someone somewhere in the world who does not deny death when it comes?

Minutes I don't remember pass. My mother gives me Robyn's number and leaves the room because I want to be alone. I make my call, getting the wrong number twice in my nervousness before I hear Robyn telling me the things I have called to hear, tentative wake and funeral arrangements, times and places for the ceremonies that are the last things we will do for Danny. I hang up the phone, thinking crazily that my mother brought me chicken because I missed dinner and now I will not feel like eating the chicken and it's a waste to throw out good food.

A waste. A loss.

If he's really gone, how come I'm still breathing?

I am in the hospital, two days after your funeral, the first admission I can remember when I do not care about chest pain or coughing or needles. I am numb. I am not interested. When I wake up in the morning I have an urgent desire to go back to bed and make the world disappear. It is the only emotion I feel strongly.

Sometimes, the outside world intrudes: A doctor comes in, bright-eyed; a nurse brings me pills. But I know better than to venture outside this room, understand what will happen if I walk down those halls. Outside, I will see you everywhere you ever were, in the halls where we raced wheelchairs and in the schoolroom where we played Monopoly. Already I am forgetting that you are not alive even while feeling your death: I hear a cough from the next room and I jump up to bring you tissues. Once today, I cut out a Garfield comic I know you'll like, twice today I half dial your phone number and expect to hear your voice. My mother goes on and on about how time heals, and I look at her as if she is speaking a language I have never learned. Nothing in the world could have prepared me for this emptiness. I don't see how a person gets used to all this pain.

It's September, the first month you haven't seen. I spend the last days of vacation cleaning up my bedroom, finding the jeans and the tapes I will want with me back at school. I turn on the record player when I pack, throwing clothes into a suitcase, and sometime later I realize I have been dancing to the beat. My energy is returning, and I am hungry again also. When I get up in the morning I can think of reasons for beginning a day. I feel it as surely as I felt your death only last month: I am climbing back to par now. I am coming back to life.

Nothing will be the same without you, ever. I will never be quite who I was before you died. But there's a world out there still, with good things in it, and I would not feel right about treasuring your short life if I wasted mine. Your dying taught me nothing so well as it taught me this: that I can cheat death every day by filling every day with life. And I want them to say of me when I die what I always said of you: that life never found me idle, that I took from every minute all it would give. Somewhere down the road, c.f. will claim me, too. But right now I'm in there fighting.

And it's the right now that counts.

6. Letters

When I remember the spring of my sophomore year at college, I suspect that I'll always
remember it as the calm before the storm.
Looking back, my only immediate concerns
in March and April centered around mid-
terms, the usual bouts with lung infection,
and whether or not I would get everything I
wanted for my twentieth birthday. I spent
that birthday in the hospital, inviting a whole
crowd of friends to the pediatrics floor for a
party and decorating my room with hand-
made signs reading "I am 20!" I still have
the photos we took during that admission,
and they speak of peace and laughter: photos
of my friend Danny standing near my wall
of birthday cards; photos of me wearing the
"I Love You" necklace my nurse Arlene delighted me with; photos of my friend Debbie
Tirado defying all traces of lung disease by
blowing up a dozen balloons in between cheers
and giggles. When I look back at those photos,
with all the advantages of hindsight, I am

struck most by how self-assured and calm I seem. The next few months were such a whirlwind of grief and ecstasy that I began to question whether I had ever known "calm" at all.

In the very last spring issue of that year's *Scholastic Voice* magazine, there appeared a questionnaire asking teachers to check off topics for future issues that might appeal to their students. *Scholastic Voice* is a magazine produced for junior high and high school students, with a circulation rate of approximately a quarter million readers — including me! I first picked up Voice sometime in junior high, and by my freshman year of high school I was a devoted fan for life. Ever eager to get criticism on my poetry and short stories, I sent the editors a few samples, promptly forgot all about it, and settled back to all the history and math homework that plagues high school students. Much later, when my submissions to Voice were only a vague memory, I was surprised by a letter from Voice's staff complimenting me on my work and telling me to look for it in an upcoming issue. As the next few years went by, there were quite a few more "upcoming issues" I had to look forward to, and later an internship offer by the Voice editors for three weeks in January. By the time my sophomore year of college rolled around, I considered the staff my friends, and when they first approached me with the idea of devoting an entire issue to my writings, I considered it just that, an offer by friends, meant to be friendly, and certainly never to amount to anything much. I was still taking everything lightly when the last Voice issue appeared, asking teachers how they would feel about a future issue dealing with the writings of a disabled student. My friends were excited, but I was matter-of-fact. My calm had not yet deserted me.

That May was the last time I was to feel complacent for many months. Sometime in late May, I took a good look at my friend Danny and forced myself to admit the undeniable. C.f. was winning its fight with him. He was tired, abysmally skinny, and just plain hurting. In my mind's eye I would always see him skateboarding on IV poles and jumping out of closets, but in the more recent past I seldom saw him out of bed. His mother and brother, who took him home and enjoyed him when he was well, probably had a more positive perspective, but I saw him only in the hospital, and only with a creeping sense of fear. On one night that haunts me still, when we were both in the hospital, Danny came into my room panting, looking for all the world as though he had just run the Boston Marathon. It took him several minutes of deep breaths before he could talk to me, and then he very casually mentioned that he was just in his room, next door, and thought he'd drop by, and was I too busy to play Monopoly? Just in his room. Just next door. His lungs were this tired from taking him 20 feet. I don't think I ever looked at Danny again without aching.

He died on August 4, while we were upstate vacationing, and even in my grief, in my anger, the irony did not escape me. August — again. While we were vacationing — again. For months afterward, even when I was able to look at Danny's death as a gift of peace after years of pain, I still felt that nagging superstition that August was out to get me and my c.f. friends, that if only Danny had lived through the month, he would have lived for years onward. A foolish thought, of course, but love isn't the only feeling apt to make fools out of people. Grief does it, too. It takes away your sense of well-being. It takes away your sense of calm, and makes you feel. That August I felt as sorry for myself as I ever hope to be, and as utterly miserable for the ones who deserved better than death. Ten days after he died, Danny would have turned 15; two weeks after that marked Juliann's second anniversary in Heaven. When I returned to school in September I remembered the easygoing Robyn of May as though she were a distant relative. I was not calm. I was reeling.

It is trite to say that time heals; trite but true. As school days went by, I found myself gaining more interest in the people around me, more interest in the coursework that piled up regularly on my desk. There was plenty of time to think of Danny, but thankfully the *world demanded some of that time. And thankfully, too, I began getting phone calls from* Voice *workers in late September, telling me they most certainly were going to do a Robyn Miller issue, and could I tell them this, correct that, help them with this other thing? Bless them — they diverted me. They kept me busy. I still missed Danny too much to think about the* Voice *issue with any real anticipation, but I was glad for the distractions. I had no way of knowing how much genuine happiness I would get from that magazine, the first happiness I felt since August.*

The November 2, 1984, issue of Scholastic Voice *magazine features me on the cover, typing at the typewriter I am using this minute, positioned over the caption "A Handicapped Teenager's Own Story." Inside, there is a letter to* Voice *readers explaining just who this Robyn character is, plus page after page of my short stories, articles, and poems. Since this issue was meant to be a theme issue, focusing on disability, the main attraction is "The Hidden Handicap," my article on "invisible" problems like chronic illness. Further along, there are pieces about people who met challenges particularly well. Some of these are stories written by me, while others are staff-written student exercises dealing with courage and positive attitudes. And deep within the magazine is a short article designed to improve letter-writing skills, inviting students to "Write a letter to Robyn!" In all fairness, I have to admit that this particular* exercise was not printed without my knowledge, as the editors and I had long ago agreed that I would try to answer whatever mail I received. "How many letters could I possibly get, anyway?" I reasoned. As it turned out, my reasoning skills left a lot to be desired. I went into the hospital just as my Voice issue hit the schools, and pretty soon I was shocked by phone calls from the Voice staff, telling me that there were 50 letters for me, 75 letters, 200 letters. Several weeks later the count hit 500. My friend Sharon down at Voice guessed the final number to be 2,500 to 3,000.

They came from all over the United States, from large cities and from farm country. They came from kids who attended expensive private schools and kids whose total school population never exceeded 50 students. They came from towns so small they sent me looking for a U.S. map, and towns so small that they weren't located on my new map. They came from kids who had never heard of cystic fibrosis in their entire lives, and from kids whose brothers, sisters, and cousins had died from it. They came from kids who had watched grandparents die from multiple sclerosis, cancer, muscular dystrophy, heart disease. They came from teenage unwed mothers. They came from teenagers serving prison sentences. They came from adults who worked for all sorts of charities and who dropped a line "just to see how you're feeling." They came with foreign stamps, from kids living in Guam, Manila, Quebec, West

Germany. And they came, all of them, addressed to me, the same girl who once complained to her friend Kenny that she had no sisters and brothers and felt like she was fighting cystic fibrosis entirely on her own.

Their numbers astonished me, but their content surprised me even more. I had not known, cynical New Yorker that I am, that so many people reach out to encourage and praise a perfect stranger. I had not known that an entire school would care enough to send Christmas cards to a person they saw on a magazine cover, tons and tons of Christmas cards for someone spending Christmas in the hospital. I read every single letter, every day while I was taking my aerosol mask, and I had not known that cheery thoughts on bright stationery would make those aerosol treatments less of a nuisance. I had not known, just a few short months before, in August, that I would ever have cause to really feel good about myself again.

The first Voice issue also did a good deal to spread the word about c.f. Every time I read a letter that began, "I never heard of cystic fibrosis before I picked up Voice . . . ," I knew that a valuable public service had been performed. I always liked writing to express what I felt, and now I was using those feelings and that writing ability to tell all the future scientists, the future doctors, the future parents, the future employers about chronic illness. Thanks to Voice, I was also allowed to spread the word through other *media forms: through a brief guest spot on a local TV talk show; through an article written about me in a local newspaper; through a Spotlight poster produced by Organon pharmaceutical company, which regularly prints posters highlighting special achievers who happen to have cystic fibrosis; through the publication of "Taking Leave" in an anthology about disabled women. When the phone rang and the mailman came during those autumn and winter days, I was almost always delighted with what I heard and read. I came to expect good news. I came to laugh more often, to get excited more often. The girl who only months before wanted to sleep all day now woke up extra early and went to bed extra late. I was at the height of emotion once again, but they were good emotions this time.*

I still missed Danny. I suspected I would forever. And it did not seem right that things in my life were suddenly going so well when his life had so abruptly ended. But as the mail poured in, I found that a huge battalion of people I'd never met stepped in to ease the loss of one small boy who'd meant so much to me. No letter was ever going to make things right, but each letter served as an impetus to take my therapy, to fight off infection, to fight back when I doubted it was worth the effort. And so that is how 3,000 perfect strangers bring you back from grief. That is how people who can't spell cystic fibrosis correctly help you beat it. That is how you keep your spirit intact when your body fails you. With a little help from your friends — that is how.

The letters printed here are samples from the mail I received in response to Voice. *As a result of this enormous and totally unexpected response, the* Voice *editors decided to devote* Voice's *April 26, 1985, issue to representative letters and my replies. Much to our amusement, this second issue did not put an end to my mail, but rather caused new letters to pour in. Though we all complained good-naturedly, I have to admit that nothing pleased me more than opening up a new batch of envelopes. I welcomed the mail, the way you welcome new friends into your house. And I print them here to introduce you to a few of my 3,000 new friends, and to remind myself, as Kenny once reminded me, that I'll never fight alone.*

Dear Robyn,

Enclosed you will find a variety of reactions to you, your writings, and cystic fibrosis. Prior to our study of the November 2 issue of <u>Voice</u>, my Language Arts classes had discussed at length the handicapped, and the various tangents which radiate from that generalized term. (We had two selections in our literature text on retardation and

physical disabilities.) Your
creations served to intensify my
students' feelings about their
perceptions of what "handicap"
actually means. And in the process,
an examination of their inner
selves naturally evolved.

You will notice that most letters
are legible and neat; you will also
detect quite easily very visible
mechanical and grammatical errors!
After the initial rough draft done
in class, students returned the
following day with a finalized copy
of their thoughts. From a
humanitarian standpoint, I felt that
to "rework" these letters would
destroy the spontaneity and honesty
of these young thinkers. Therefore,
all letters have been read by me for
content approval only. Yes, from an
English teacher's perspective, these
letters are . . . well — shall I say
lacking? Lacking in many ways except
one — genuineness.

So my apologies to you and the
English language! But more
important, my appreciation to one
who is such an inspiration to those
of us who daily take life for
granted. . . .

Sincerely,
Mrs. Mary Ellen Smith
Virginia

Dear Mrs. Smith,

I have just read the letters from your class and I feel that I owe you a personal thank you. You would not believe how many letters I received from kids, on top of which their teachers actually wrote corrections or their grade for the assignment. I was so upset to see these teachers totally miss the point of the *Voice* issue. That issue was meant to generate feelings and thoughts and honesty and candor, not to encourage kids to get their spelling down pat or perfect their grammar. Every time I read a letter from a student who poured out his heart to me and whose thoughts were edited and corrected in red pen, I felt sick. Obviously, those kids knew a great deal more than their instructors, and the whole situation struck me as pretty sad. How do you grade a feeling anyway? Couldn't those teachers have saved the punctuation lesson for another day?

Obviously, your kids are lucky enough to have a teacher who knows when to put content first. I am so very glad that you did not "rework" the letters, as they meant more to me with all the errors in them. I sensed the most genuineness and the most love in those letters written by students whose teachers were smart enough to let the writer speak for himself. This is what you have done, and this is what your students have done, and the results warmed my heart. The letters are not lacking in *anything*. Good spelling, after all, can be picked up anytime, but honesty is something you have to catch when you can.

Although I can never answer all your kids, I did pick out one or two letters from the pile. Please understand that I received (much to my astonishment) close to 3,000 letters, and they're still coming in. I wish I could answer all of them!

Thank you for your compliments and for using *Voice* in your classroom. I am a better person for having met you and your kids, if only on paper.

Take care of yourself,
Robyn Miller

Dear Robyn,

Hi! How are you doing? I am doing just fine. The reason I am writing is because I just read a little bit of your life story in the book called "Voice". Here is a little bit of my life story; I am 13 years of age, and I am in the 8th grade.

The main point that touched me was when you said "that it is hard lossing someone that you realy love". I know how you feel! My dad's in the Army and we move from place to place every three years or so. I have lost a lot of people that I realy cared about too. I know its hard but just keep your chin up and go on with your life. You only have

so many years to live, so you better
enjoy it while you can.

I hope you enjoyed my short
letter. Don't let no one put you
down, because no one is better then
you are.

Take care!!

You Pen-Pal Friend,
Marisol
Germany

Dear Marisol,

I really enjoyed your letter and those from
your classmates. It was exciting to hear from
people who had done so much traveling so
early in life! When your classmates told me
about the different countries in which they
had lived, it made me green with envy, since
I haven't been to many exciting places myself.
Someday you could write a book about all
your adventures!

Of course, as you mentioned, being on the
move a lot has disadvantages, too, maybe
especially for teenage girls who like to settle
down in one place long enough to go to school
and have one special boyfriend, etc. And it
must be hard also to leave a house you've
spent any amount of time in, since it doesn't
take most people too long to feel sentimental
about a certain room in a certain home in a
certain town. I think I might have trouble
coping with this at first, but who knows, it
might end up making me a stronger person.

You seem to have made a pretty good adjustment.

As for leaving friends behind when your family moves on, I guess there are two ways you can look at it. Either you can lament the fact that you've lost so many friends, or you can be grateful for the amount of time you had with each person. One other thing to keep in mind is that you probably appreciate your friends and the value of friendship more than most teenagers, because you've had to leave so many people behind during your life. I'll bet you don't take friendship for granted, and that's a pretty good attribute!

Right now, I am trying to follow my own advice and be thankful for whatever time I get with some of my sicker friends. Sometimes I am selfish and want more time with them on earth, but hopefully I'll always remember how lucky I've been to know them at all. You are right, of course, in saying that we'd better enjoy life while we can, because time certainly has a way of passing by more quickly than we like to think. And I know that I for one wouldn't want to die without first making something out of my life! People think they'll get innumerable shots at life, but no one does. Now, if only I could always remember that!

Thank you for writing to encourage me and thank you for sharing your feelings with me. I liked meeting Marisol!

Love from your friend,
Robyn Miller

Dear Robyn,

I am a 7th grader.

I have just finished reading your article in "Voice." I feel like I have taken life for granted after that. I wonder what it would be like to be like you? After the article I also feel inspired. I know that people, handicapped or not, can do things if they really try.

My teacher says someday you might die but you are determined to live. I think you can and will love and be a great writer.

I know being in and out of the hospital wouldn't be much fun, but if that is what it takes to live, you have to do it.

Sincerely,
Chris
Virginia

Dear Chris,

I really appreciate all the nice compliments, however undeserved they might be! It was a joy to hear from you and from your classmates. I can't answer everyone's letter, but I will try to answer a few, and I hope you forgive me for the ones I cannot respond to. I really was overwhelmed by mail in the last few months, and even though I enjoy reading the letters, it seems there's no way to write replies to each one! But please know that every letter meant a great deal to me — that's not just your standard polite talk, I really mean it!

I am glad that you got a better sense of people's capabilities after reading *Voice*, because that was one of the purposes of the magazine. You seem to have learned very well that everyone has certain strong points and certain weak points, and that disability has little to do with this. As you say, all people, disabled or not, "can do things if they really try." Of course, some things might take a little ingenuity, such as modifying a room so that a person who uses a wheelchair can easily reach the sink, the closets, and so forth. Society could probably do a great deal more to help disabled people along these lines — for example, by making buses and trains accessible to people using wheelchairs, crutches, and other aids. With a little inventiveness, there's probably very little that disabled people cannot participate in. In some ways, I'm afraid, disabled people have more trouble from the society that they live in than they do from their own disability. For example, a disabled person using a wheelchair can enjoy a theater performance as much as a nondisabled person — *if* the theater's architects and managers make doorways and aisles wide enough for a wheelchair. And as for me, my cough and shortness of breath never stopped me from enjoying a good museum exhibit, but what if the museum doesn't have working elevators, or doesn't have a rule about smoking? We need more legislation that considers the needs and the rights of disabled people. This is not even an "adult" problem, exclusively — for example, my junior high school and my elementary school weren't fully accessible to disabled students, and I'd bet you've attended schools like this, too, without realizing it!

You also seemed to get a good grasp of another theme mentioned in *Voice* — the importance of determination. Your teacher put the problem to you very well, and very honestly, when she said that I might die but that I am fighting to live. She is right on both counts, and you are right in feeling that people must do everything possible to survive, until hope is gone. That takes guts, Chris, more than I've got sometimes, but a good attitude and a lot of determination really does help a person in any struggle. You might not win the fight in the end, but you certainly won't win if you give up before you try or in midstream. I want to die trying.

And as for the poem you wrote about me — it's great, and I'm flattered! Your poem did what poems are supposed to do; it made me feel, and that is a remarkable gift. Thank you for considering me someone who, as you say in your poem, won't give up — I certainly won't, not when I have friends like you cheering me on!

Thanks for sharing,
Robyn Miller

Dear Robyn,

I have a similar experiance to
yours. I had braces put on and
everyone thought sometimes I wasn't
really going to the orthodonist, but
trying to miss school. My braces
were also correcting another problem
about me, swallowing my spit with a
slurping sound. The class calls me
slurp and I hate it. I thank you for
giving me a reason to fight back.

Your friend,
Kyle
Georgia

Dear Kyle,

Thanks so very much for sharing your
problem with me. It took a lot of guts to discuss it with a stranger, and I think you're
really special for being able to talk so openly!
One of the qualities I like best is honesty.

I wore braces myself for a short time, so I
can relate to the teasing you encountered. I'll
bet everyone who has ever worn braces has
heard his or her share of "metal mouth" and
"tinsel teeth" remarks! It's hard to put up
with that at the same time that you're putting up with the discomfort of having all
those weird wires in your mouth! But keep
your chin up, they'll be off before you know
it, and all your friends will feel pretty dumb
for having made fun of you once they see
those nice straight teeth!

As for the kids who call you slurp, I don't

blame you for hating the whole situation. They sound pretty insensitive and not all that smart, either. Anyone with brains could figure out that swallowing your spit with a slurping sound is not your fault and that you don't like it any more than anyone else does. People can be so dumb sometimes! If I were you, I think I would try to explain the problem once to the kids, without getting mad or upset. Maybe they're just teasing you because they don't understand the problem and are scared it might happen to them. But after this explanation, if they still tease you, I would ignore them. Maybe someday they'll grow up! Right now they are acting like two-year-olds. They are really not worthy of your concern, Kyle.

I'm glad the *Voice* articles gave you a reason to stand up for your rights. Just don't let anyone make you think that you are a less worthy person because of your problems. I'm sure you know better than that. You sound okay to me!

Kyle, I am glad to call you my friend.

Take care,
Robyn Miller

Dear Robyn,
    It is about 9:20 on the day of the 1st of November. I have just finished reading the articale about you in Scholastic. I hope that you are feeling fine. I am so happy to

read about another handicap person
fighting thier problem.

I am a 3LD studient. I have what
is call Deslexicia, it is a problem
of my mind. I read letters
backwords. I have about learned how
to make my self to change them on
enpulse. The funny part is that my
doctor's and Sycologist said that I
was not going to be able to do all
that I wanted to do. Thy said that
I would never be able to read on my
level of grade in fact thy said
that I wouldn't read pass 5th grade
level. I am now a 10th grader and
reading on 7th level. In 1982 I
wrote and directed a play called
"the Triumph" about a deaf girl who
learned to dance and handle her
handicap. My 8th grade chorus class
put it on.

I am some times afriad to let
people know I am handicap. But after
reading your story, I and feeling
better about it.

> Your handicap
> Friend
> Ronald
> Florida

Dear Ronald,

I am going to save your letter forever, because it made my whole day. It was certainly

one of the best letters I've read, and remember, my mail from *Voice* is now numbering up there in the thousands. But nobody moved me the way you did.

I know lots of people at my college with dyslexia and other forms of learning disabilities, and though they have their share of problems they *are* attending college and they *are* doing very well. So you see, there is every reason to think that you will do just fine in high school and that you can go on as far as you want with your education. Don't let anyone tell you differently! Already you have gone beyond the expectations of several doctors and a psychologist, who obviously didn't know what you can do if you set your mind to it! All your life you're going to meet people who doubt that you can do this or that because of your disability, and it will be up to you to prove them wrong by accomplishing everything you feel capable of and by feeling good about yourself. If you want to do something, just go for it, Ronald, and don't worry about the doubters. I know you can make it, because you're already on the right track.

Your letter told me a lot about the importance of determination, a force that apparently is very strong in your life. Good — that puts you one step ahead of everyone else. There are lots of people out there to whom everything comes easy, people who don't have to work hard to get what they want. I don't know how you feel about this, but I feel sorry for those people because they're missing out on a lot. Those 7th grade reading scores of yours wouldn't mean so much to you, would they, if you didn't have to fight so hard for them? And as for me, my grades at school mean more to me because I am absent so often and have to work so hard to catch up. Imagine how boring life would be if you didn't have to struggle for anything! Of course, we all get tired of working so hard every so often, but still, it sure beats having everything handed over to you, doesn't it? Those reading scores don't just mean you can read well, they also mean you are a fighter who knows how to work for his success! Even if your reading scores never go any higher, you're way ahead of the people who read easily and take it for granted.

I was very interested in hearing about the play you wrote, since I have always loved reading and watching plays. You must be pretty talented to have written something so good that your class wanted to put it on! I'll bet you were proud of yourself, with good reason. The topic sounds pretty thought-provoking, too, and I'll bet a lot of people are now more in touch with the problems of handling disability after having seen "The Triumph." I wish I could have been there to applaud!

I know it's scary to admit that you have a disability, because lots of people won't understand that dyslexia does not make you a "different" person, only one who approaches reading and writing slightly differently. But I think that once you explain to your teachers and your friends just what your problem involves, they really will understand. In fact, they'll probably think more of you for trying so hard and for doing so well. And you should feel pretty good about that, too.

I am glad that *Voice* helped you feel better about your problem. Your letter did a lot for me, too.

Take care!
Love,
Robyn Miller

P.S. Please don't call yourself my "handi-capped friend." You are just my friend Ron-ald. Your disability is simply not the most important thing about you.

Dear Robyn,
My name is Karen, I'm a grade 8 student, and I have a cousin who has Spinalbifit. He's always grouchy and hard to get along with, I don't know if it's because he's feeling sorry for himself or what. I just wanted to know if you think people find it a bit hard to get along with you, do you wish when you're having an attack that someone else could have your pain, and do you think

there will ever be a cure for Cystic
Fibrosis?

P.S. I hope you're feeling well!

Sincerely,
Karen
Canada

Dear Karen,

I didn't know that *Voice* reached Canada,
so imagine my surprise when I saw the en-
velope from your class! I have been delighted
in the past few months to get mail from quite
a few places outside of the U.S., and it really
intrigues me because I've hardly done any
traveling at all myself. I did go to Old Quebec
once, and I loved every minute of it. Your
country must be magnificent if all the cities
are anything like that one. Someday perhaps
I'll see Ontario for myself!

In your letter you ask some pretty tough
questions, but I'll try to be as honest in my
answers as you were in your questions. I'll
start with the second question first, if you
don't mind: Do I ever wish someone else
could have my pain? Well, I suppose sometimes I'd like to get rid of c.f., but I don't
think I'd want to give it to somebody else. I'd
rather that it was cured for good so that *nobody* suffered with it. I must admit that there
have been times when I've met particularly
insensitive people and I've wanted to give
them c.f. for only a few hours, to show them
what it's like, but I don't think I could wish
c.f. on anyone for any length of time. It just

wouldn't be fair to do that, knowing full well how much pain can be involved in this disease. It's pretty tempting though, at times — giving c.f. to someone would teach that person compassion pretty quickly! It might even teach those poor fools who go around complaining about such terrible tragedies as a hangnail that they have an awful lot to be grateful for. But in the end, c.f. is too high a price to pay for learning those lessons.

Next question: Do I think people find it hard to get along with me? Well, sure, probably, but it doesn't necessarily have to do with c.f.! Sometimes when a friend of mine is sick or when I am tired of being in the hospital, I can be a pretty obnoxious person, as anyone who knows me will tell you! But sometimes I have days when I'm just grouchy, the same as everyone else, and c.f. isn't a factor at all. I wondered when I read your letter whether spina bifida is the cause of your cousin's bad moods or whether he's just going through some problems right now that make him cross. He might be feeling sorry for himself, but maybe he's having difficulties of an entirely different kind. You can try to be pleasant, but to be honest, I wouldn't blame myself for any arguments I had with a person who was so hard to get along with. Spina bifida or not, he has to live in the world, and he's going to have lots more problems if he lives with an unpleasant attitude. This is not to make light of spina bifida and the problems it entails; this is just to say that there are plenty of friendly, happy people in the world who happen to have spina bifida, and your cousin could probably do better if he developed an attitude like theirs. Maybe in time he will feel better about himself and then he'll be nicer to everyone else also.

And for your last question: Do I think there will ever be a cure for c.f.? Yes, I do, although I'm pretty sure I won't live to see it, since they're just now beginning to make some headway into the really tricky questions about the disease. I have seen some progress made in my lifetime, and I hope to see some more, but I don't think I'll live long enough to see the final victory. But I *know* that they will nevertheless reach that victory someday, and I am so glad of that!

Thank you for your letter and for challenging me to think.

Sincerely,
Robyn Miller

Dear Ms. Miller:
You have a lot of courage telling people how you feel. I'm glad that you wrote about your illness. I never heard about CF before. If I meet anyone with it I won't be afraid of them, and I'll understand a little bit what they are going through, thanks to your writing on it and expressing how you feel.

Did any of your friends at school

not talk to you after they found out
you had CF? Do some people think
that they can get it from you?

How can you put up with people who
say that CF is just a way of getting
attention like the professor.

Do you wish sometimes that you
weren't even born? I don't know what
I would do if I found out I had an
incurable illness.

You are so brave and talented; I
wish that I had courage like you and
could always look on the bright side
of things. I'm glad that I read your
articles on CF.

Sincerely yours
Lynn
Wisconsin

Dear Lynn,

I really enjoyed your letter and I thank you
so much for taking the time to care, and to
write. I'm way behind in answering *Voice*
mail due to the many letters received, but I'm
trying to catch up! Lucky thing my typewriter and I get along so well, or I'd be having a miserable time!

In your letter, you touched on an important
theme — honesty — and I really appreciate
the fact that you picked up the honesty in
that magazine. You wrote that it is coura-
geous to tell people how one feels, and, of
course, you're right, it does take a certain
amount of guts to "go public." But I do not

believe I have other options. I feel that other people will pick up my example, and will be as comfortable or as uneasy about my illness as I am. If I tell the truth, the good parts and the bad, in a very frank manner, people are bound to pick up my cue and act matter-of-factly about my problems. So many of my c.f. friends hide their illness from people, but I know my (healthy) friends are made of fine stuff and can discuss a problem openly. If you tell the truth, people relax. And you see, there are fringe benefits — you said yourself that after reading *Voice* you won't be afraid of c.f. patients, should you meet any. Good for you!

I can't think of a single friend who avoided me once they understood my condition. Of course, some strangers hear my cough and think it's contagious, and avoid me for fear of catching it, so the first thing I always make known about c.f. is that it is entirely non-contagious. After that, everyone calms down. I have a few friends who can't cope with the hardest aspects of c.f., like death, but that's okay, because I'm not entirely sure how well *I'd* cope with a friend's terminal illness, if I were healthy. You have to try to understand the other person's perspective.

And now, you ask, do I wish that I'd never been born? Never. Sometimes, when I get extremely frustrated, I say in frustration, "I wish I was dead!" but the feeling always passes. When you have an incurable sickness, you generally just hope for lots of time and relatively good health to enjoy it. You cope. And you hope. And Lynn, that's exactly what you'd do if you had c.f., believe me. You think you couldn't handle it, but you could. What choice do you have, really? You want to live, so you fight. It's that simple. And that hard.

I am glad, like you, that you had a chance to read *Voice* and learn a little more about cystic fibrosis. I see that you have gained from it, and I am happy for us both. Thank you for all the compliments and for sharing your thoughts with me!

Much health and happiness to you.

Your new friend
Robyn

Dear Robyn

Hi, my name is Sean and I'm an 8th grader.

My English teacher has a regular subscription to <u>Voice</u> and asked us to read the 3 or 4 articles written by you in the November issue of <u>Voice</u>. So, that Saturday I went out on the patio and read the article(s). I don't know anyone with CF so I didn't really know the details of the disability.

I don't think any of us know how fortunate we are, but you helped us see that we are fortunate. I don't know if it will make us change any of our physical ways, but it will

definitely be lodged in our minds
and make us thank God that we are
fortunate and can help, with our
money, to find a soon-coming cure
for your disability.

I hope this letter will also help
you see that we, all, really do care
and want to help all the people with
C.F. I also want you to know that
you've got about 60 eight-graders
praying for you. Well, I really do
admire your courage and
determination. And I want to say
"thanks" for helping us see into the
minds of people with C.F. Thanks
again.

A New Friend,
Sean
Alabama

Dear Sean,

I received your letter and I'm sorry for the
delay in answering. Believe me, if I didn't
have so much mail you would have heard
from me a lot sooner, because your letter
really stirred me to respond. I am so glad that
you had the opportunity to read *Voice* and
that I have the opportunity to meet you — if
only on paper!

First of all, you are not alone in having
never heard of c.f. before. Most of the people
who wrote to me didn't know the details of
the disease until they read my work in *Voice*.
Believe it or not, there are a lot of doctors out

there who never heard of c.f. either, even though so many people have the disease and so many more are carriers of it. There are hundreds upon hundreds of people with c.f., and that means that many families will be touched by it. So you see, it is a good thing that you now know more about the sickness, because someday a friend of yours might tell you he has it; or perhaps someone close to you will give birth to a child with c.f. With any luck, the disease will be wiped out before you are an adult, but it still doesn't hurt to be prepared. One of the things I am most thankful for is that *Voice* educated a lot of people who otherwise would have been unclear as to what cystic fibrosis is and what it involves.

You also touched on a second important function of the *Voice* issue: bringing home to people how lucky they really are. Even though I am sick myself, it often takes a lot to remind me that in many ways I am extremely fortunate. There is a saying I am very fond of: "I felt sorry for myself because I had no shoes until I met a man who had no feet." I think even the sickest person can find something to be grateful for. Of course, you wouldn't want to turn into a Pollyanna, counting your blessings constantly and being sickeningly optimistic. But it sure brightens your outlook to take a look around once in a while and see how much better you have it than lots of other people. I have personally learned to be plenty grateful from my contact in the hospital with kids who are so much sicker than I am. I remember very well one night in the hospital when I was feeling particularly sorry for myself because I wouldn't be going home for at least two weeks. Then I passed the room of a friend of mine who was dying of cancer, and it struck me that *she* wouldn't be going home at all. Boy, I cleaned up my self-pity act fast. Sometimes it takes a strong reminder to tell you how lucky you really are.

I also want to thank you for all your words of encouragement. I am glad to hear that, in your words, you "want to help all the people with c.f." You have already helped one person with c.f. by taking the time to share your thoughts with her. And there are lots of other ways to help people with c.f.: There are fund-raising events all the time, and your local c.f. chapter can tell you how to get involved. I've done a few bowl-a-thons for c.f. myself, and besides being lots of fun, they left me with the feeling that I was helping lots of other sicker people, which is of course a pretty good feeling!

Your prayers and those of the other eighth-graders are much, much appreciated! They may not get me better faster, but it sure is nice going to bed every night knowing that so many people are rooting for me. I cannot find words to thank you enough.

Sean, thanks again for writing. I am proud to call you my friend!

Take care,
Robyn Miller

7. Attitudes

One day several years ago, a well-meaning hospital worker approached me and my friend Michael as we sat talking in his hospital room. As our discussion turned to an extremely weak friend of ours with cancer, the worker clucked his tongue, shook his head sadly, and said that he knew the youngster and felt sorry for him. Knowing that our friend's personality invited more admiration than pity, Mike and I both began to protest. After all, we argued, the boy was bright, spirited, and very brave; pretty impressive qualities for any person of any age. Mike in particular got extremely annoyed with the worker, explaining over and over that condescension never helped anyone. "But you must realize," the man said dramatically, "that your little friend is half dead." Mike met his eyes. "And you must realize that our little friend is half alive."

What Michael and my little friend with cancer both shared was a positive attitude, or at least the knowledge that attitude can make or break an already shaky situation. Michael knew that fighting for your life takes tremendous energy, energy that must be renewed daily because the disease renews itself daily. In order to keep that supply of willpower, in order to find reasons to take another round of chemotherapy or cough up another mucus plug in an endless succession of mucus plugs, you have to imagine that something good is inherent in the struggle, or that something good will come out of the struggle, or that the end of the struggle might well be in sight. You have to lie to yourself if necessary. You have to consider life long-term, and know that this one therapy session may be the key factor in your staying well or your spending half of July in the hospital. You have to find reason to continue, when continuing is not your easiest or most pleasant option. You have to see someone as half alive when all the world sees him as half dead.

My little friend with cancer understood this intuitively. He was never a Pollyanna, but he had a remarkable gift for grasping all that was horribly wrong with his body while enjoying all that was right and hoping that all would get better. He hated IV needles in his hand, but I noticed he learned quickly to color one-handed. He could not attend regular school, but he made me ashamed of myself with his eagerness to attend the hospital school and with his constant inquiries as to what this or that word meant. He grew too

138

weak to walk, but he made steering motions with his thin arms and announced to me that he was riding his bicycle. He made the best of things, and believe me, he had very little to work with here. He lived the hardest life I have ever known, but he lived it well.

I am not that gifted. Many times Dr. Doyle has heard me shout that if I really do live to be 25 or even 30, it will be a curse rather than a blessing. I mean it when I say it, but I do not feel this way for any length of time. When one complication after another sets into my lungs, it is very easy to become frustrated and to momentarily give in to that frustration. Then, too, the person with c.f. is living with a progressive disease, with the knowledge that the disease will never go away and will get worse instead of better. If things look awful now, what will they be like when I have lung damage, less weight to fight back with, more complications? It is thinking like this that sends me shouting angrily to Dr. Doyle, who wisely keeps quiet out of her knowledge that my anger is justified and that I do not feel so angry most of the time. An occasional screaming match, aimed more at cystic fibrosis than at Dr. Doyle, helps defuse the anger that, I hope, lies for the most part under a positive outlook on life.

"Positive," of course, is relative. I do not feel upbeat about my chances of being the first c.f. patient ever to die from old age. I do not feel positive that I will wake up tomorrow without any trace of lung disease. I do not feel positive that I will live long enough to see a cure for this particular lung disease, misunderstood and hopelessly baffling as it is. If I wasted my energies developing a positive attitude about these impossibilities, I would wither away within minutes. I cannot mentally afford to pin my hopes on a cure for cystic fibrosis this coming Thursday at two o'clock. So, when people ask me if I am optimistic about cystic fibrosis and about my future with it, I always try to find out what they mean by optimistic. If their definition of optimistic is of the cure-at-the-end-of-the-rainbow variety, I would have to say that I am not optimistic at all.

But, of course, this does not mean that I am entirely pessimistic either. It does not mean that I stopped doing aerosol treatments long ago because I figured they would not ultimately come to much good. It does not mean that at the first sign of worsened lung infection, I take off for California instead of the hospital, believing that if I am dying my doctors could not save me anyway. It does not mean that I do not attend school or think about holding a job, because, after all, I'll be dead long before retirement age. It means only that I am practical about my chances, that I gather information carefully in order to best understand those chances, that I understand all that might go wrong but still work at finding reasons to make things go right, because, after all, there must be something in life worth doing an aerosol treatment or another hour of therapy for. I want to find those highlights. I want to make them work for me. Cystic fibrosis experts may call that ludicrous, but I call that a positive attitude. And I want to keep it forever.

I know all the benefits of a positive attitude largely because my attitude as a teenager was far more negative. I recall being 16, concerned with body image and boys' opinions, and thinking that my life was awful because sometimes I had black and blue IV marks on my hands. I remember being 17 and being certain that taking five erythromycin pills daily was the worst fate in the world, never dreaming that four years later I'd gladly take them if only they did some good. I recall thinking that I was the sickest person I'd ever known, the most "different" person in high school, the most miserable person to exist in a very long time. And, of course, looking back, I can see how that negativity harmed me. Physically, I was much the worse for making grim predictions about my life, because those predictions sometimes led to a harmful, rebellious attitude. If I wasn't going to live to be married, to have a job and a child and all my dreams fulfilled, why bother taking care of an already failing body? I cannot count how many IV needles I ripped out of my arm on this premise. I cannot count how many therapy sessions I refused. Only when my knowledge about cystic fibrosis increased, when I gained an understanding of what I could reasonably expect, did my attitude grow more positive and my behavior shape up. Part of this rebellion, I am sure, was normal teen-age cutting-of-the-apron-strings, but part was simply fear and ignorance as to what could be gained from following my medical regimen. Even now, years after my outlook has considerably improved, I look back on all those wasted days and feel regret. I know that my present attitude is the only one I can work with, but I still wonder how much lung capacity I lost when I lost my sense of the positive.

There are, of course, even today, factors that work against my positive attitude. The worst of these is my own fear, my own creeping sense of alarm as once again, regardless of the amount of medical care I've received, some setback occurs and I am back to square one. It is so hard to be positive when you are coughing up blood for the fourth straight day. It is so hard to be positive when a friend whose c.f. was moderately mild dies without justice and without any logical cause. It is so hard to keep a bright outlook on the future when you constantly read statistics telling you that you have already outlived half of the people born with cystic fibrosis and face slim chances of living into your thirties, your forties, your eighties. And it is so hard to be positive when you not only face fears but face them alone, because the people you shared your fears with most openly, the people most likely to understand, have already lost their battles to cystic fibrosis. I can fight any *medical complication with a positive view-point, but it is harder to be positive when fighting an unnamed, unknown, nagging sense of fear about my own future. There is no medicine for fear. I cannot cheer myself up by telling myself that Dr. Mayer will pre-scribe four pills three times a day to make me less afraid. And so it is when I am most frightened that I am most negative.*

And when I am most impatient. Sometimes I think that my attitude toward cystic fibrosis would be more positive if I lived in a vacuum, or at least in a world where people did not shake their heads sadly at me or avoid me for fear of catching my disease. I remember very well one incident last year when I walked into a neighborhood grocery store on a night when my cough was pretty heavy. I was well armed with tissues and perfectly able to take care of myself, but a young stock boy nevertheless complained to me about "that disgusting cough." Despite the fact that I took more care in my explanations to him than I normally do, he would not be convinced that my cough was not contagious and that he had no right to hassle me on the basis of my medical prob-lems. I eventually left the store, having temporarily shut him up, but I felt terribly vulnerable and underconfident in public situa-tions for several weeks afterward. Was everyone staring? Were people making nasty remarks about my cough under their breath? Would I have to explain myself for the rest of my life? My sense of the upbeat, of well-

being, deserts me when these questions begin to press. I sometimes believe that I would dwell less often and less negatively on cystic fibrosis if the rest of the world followed suit. All positive attitudes abandon me when people constantly bring up everything that is negative about my life.

Fortunately, I have friends who remind me by their own examples that a positive attitude is worth working at. The first story that follows is about the young cancer patient Michael and I discussed that long-ago day, the one whose determination and cheerfulness made Mike and me feel that he was not half dead but half alive. Although names and certain details have been changed, I have tried to capture in full detail the optimism that this child possessed and that he helped me develop myself. The second piece is entirely fiction, but it, too, deals with attitude and perspective, examining the different ways a teenage girl comes to view her new stepfather. Although she originally dwells on all the negative aspects of their relationship, her position becomes more tolerant as she thinks about the pluses as well as the minuses. I have titled this story "Steps," but the title is not only a reference to stepfamilies. It is also a statement of my belief that I can take steps toward becoming a more optimistic person, even when disease steps in to play games with my life.

Dear Alex

Dear Alex,

I'm waiting for you to die. A stranger wouldn't know; a stranger would think I'm watching television, turning the channels to the *Honeymooners* special. A stranger would think I am having a good time. But then a stranger wouldn't know that I am looking more toward the telephone than the television, because as much as I don't want the call, I want to be the one who answers the phone.

Of course, I do not expect it to ring just yet. Not now, not in the middle of *The Best of The Honeymooners*, the show you stay up for past your bedtime every night. I didn't always know what you did, alone, those nights in the hospital, but just a few months ago I began to find out. Just a few months ago on a day when you and I were both sick, I sat talking to a friend by the nurses' station, and watching you. I like watching you, Alex, even when it hurts, even that day when your skeleton-skinny body sat in a wheelchair propped up on pillows. To distract myself, probably, to take my mind off your bones, I talked loudly and deliberately to my friend about TV shows. I liked the older comedies best, yes, I liked *All in the Family*, certainly *Bob Newhart*, too, and how about *The Honeymooners*? Oh, I love *The Honeymooners*, I enthused. I love Ralph Kramden. And I went on like that, cheerleading, until I heard your little raspy voice. "I like *The Honeymooners*, too." That's what you said, and I nearly fell off my chair. How would you know about *The Honeymooners*? You were only seven years old! Didn't seven-year-olds like *Sesame Street* and *Mister Rogers*? Didn't seven-year-olds go to bed long before *The Honeymooners* came on, especially sick seven-year-olds, especially sick and hospitalized and cancer-ridden seven-year-olds? "I like *The Honeymooners*," you told me. "I like when Ralph screams, 'Hey, Alice!'" And though you made me laugh, your small voice imitating Ralph's bellow, I walked away feeling struck, knowing more about you than I'd known. So that's what you did, lying in bed by yourself. You couldn't see anymore, because of the tumors, but you watched television. You stayed up every night to watch TV. If anyone had asked, I would have said you'd known more than your share of tragedy, and here you were, every night, watching comedy on TV.

You wouldn't die in the middle of *The Honeymooners*, would you, Alex? You wouldn't be in pain now, still, as I watch a show that made you laugh? I saw you today with advance warning from Dr. Thomas, and even so I was not prepared for your pain. "People are walking out of Alex's room looking sad," Dr. Thomas had said. His words should have alerted me. No one is ever sad after a visit with you, just relaxed after spending another half hour coloring, or giggling after listening to your seven-year-old mouth sprout 30-year-old thoughts. "Why are you watching the news?" a friend once asked you. "Why aren't you watching cartoons?" And you looked up at your friend and you said with no little impatience, "Oh, Rhonda, I'm improving my mind!" I laughed when they told me that, Alex, the way I laughed when you inquired after Steve, a young patient who'd just been operated on. Steve, someone told you, was feeling tired and sick, because he'd run around only one day after his operation. And what did you say, all seven years of you, when we gave you this report? "Well," you replied gravely, "I *told* Steve you have to take it easy after surgery." People laughed with you, Alex, even when they didn't intend to, even when they walked into your room feeling sick or sad or tired. Every day people walked out of your room feeling healthier in spirit, but today people walk out of your room aching all over.

And not for lack of encouragement, either. We clutch each other in the halls, we people who have watched you grow up, and we go over and over all the slights that you have suffered. "His pain is awful," we tell each other, "and it goes on and on." We pinpoint all of them, Alex, each of your particular hurts. We have been holding back too long, suffering with you in silence, but now we egg each other on, talking about everything from your lack of hair to your lack of breath. To your lack of tears. Yes, this, too, because — did I mention it? — you are the only one not crying now. You hurt, and you press your fingers to the stomach where a tumor bulges visibly, but you do not cry for yourself anymore. A doctor comes to see you and even now she must pull teeth, getting you to tell her where you ache, if you ache. "Alex, can you hear me? Does anything hurt?" But you shake your head no, and then you amend your answer — "No, thank you." It amazes me that you use what little air is left you to express gratitude.

And what did I say to you, Alex, when I saw you? Not much that mattered. Not much that a seven-year-old could take for his own, to use when he needed something so badly to hold on to. Part of me, Alex, wanted suddenly to be your priest, even though I am not a great believer and may well never be one if I continue to stand near dying Alexes. But still, part of me wanted to tell you all would be all right, to make sure that you understand that better things were promised you. But I kept silent, more out of your needs than my own, because it was horribly apparent to everyone that you wanted to live. You were still fighting, Alex, even when the effort cost you, even when your nurse and I wondered out loud what you had left to fight for. So I didn't comfort you with words about Heaven, Alex, not while you clung so hard to everything that was here and now. But to myself I pleaded with you a hundred times: You can let go now. You can go.

Remember when they wanted to put the

tube down your nose, Alex? You were so small, so undernourished, and they had no other way of feeding you. But you cried when Dr. Kay came into your room with all the equipment, even though you had no sight left to see how long and scary that tube really was. I had thought that your tears were from fear of getting hurt, and Dr. Kay also assumed you did not want the tube because you did not want the pain. But when I coaxed Dr. Kay into leaving the room for a minute, I found out just what about the tube bothered you most. They connect the nose tube to bags of liquid food hanging on an iv pole, and it seems you were mostly worried about the height of the pole. "Oh, Robyn," you said, "if I get that tube put in, Daddy won't have room for me and the big pole in his car. If I get the tube put in, how can I go home?" I swallowed a few times before I touched that question, Alex, because to look at you one knew right away that you would never again go home, IV pole or not. To look at you one would understand that you were in the hospital for good these days. But you wanted to live, to live at home with Daddy and Mommy, and so you fought hard for life and fought any tubes or contraptions that might keep you in the hospital. And I thought about that day, Alex, this morning when I saw you, when I told you that *now*, now finally, you could give up trying and we'd understand. Now, finally, you could let go if you wanted, and no one would hold it against you that you stopped the fight.

Except that you are not ready to die yet, Alex. I called the hospital an hour after I'd left your side, and there you still were, they told me, amazing everyone on the floor. Quite a few people were on the floor today, actually, because your best hospital friend called everyone she knew would want to say good-bye. So when I got to the hospital I wasn't the only one trying to find words to say in your room; the nurses were there, too, from all over, and all the doctors, and the cleaning ladies. Oh, Alex, it just about broke my heart seeing those cleaning ladies. How could such a small boy find so many friends? I remember when you celebrated your seventh birthday in the hospital, and everyone you loved made you a special "big boy's" party. I was admitted to the hospital just a week after that, and one night after I had read you your bedtime story I found your birthday cards in a drawer. Twenty or 30 birthday cards at the least, Alex, and from people you wouldn't think would be particularly interested in one little boy. After all, there were lots of sick kids in the hospital, and they celebrated birthdays on the floor all the time. But those cards in your drawer proved that your seventh birthday stood apart from all the rest: "To Alex, Love, Dr. Duncan," the cards read, "To Alex from the nurses who like his smile" . . . "To Alex from his friends in the gift shop." I stopped at that one, Alex, to wipe away tears, because so far as I know you were too weak to have ever set foot in the gift shop. Oh, Alex, how did you make friends you'd never even met? Could we bottle it, Alex, whatever kind of charm was your secret? Could we hang it on a wall somewhere, so that the next time we read about wars and hatred in the newspapers, we'll remember?

Who stayed with you, Alex, after I left you today? The nurses told me your mother sat near you for hours, leaving only when she was relieved by your father who had just come. It's hard for them, Alex, with other small kids at home, but from my own biased viewpoint I hope they're with you when you die. We talked about it once, your favorite hospital friend and I, and it turns out we both say the same prayers every night. "Please, God," we say, "let Alex die in his sleep, without pain. But if he has to die in the daytime, God, couldn't You see to it that someone is with him when he goes?" And tonight, Alex, I fear your aloneness even more than I fear your death. Is that because you once told me how much you feared your aloneness, too? Reading you stories and playing you record albums one night, it was at least one A.M. before I started off to my own room. And even then your tiny voice followed me to the door — did I have to go now, and why, and couldn't I stay just a little longer? I had expected you, quick-minded as you were, to concoct a thousand reasons why I should stay, but you stopped me dead in my tracks with the simplest explanation I'd ever heard. "Alex, you know I have to go," I told you. "But, Robyn," you'd answered, "I just don't want to be alone."

What's it like, Alex, to be living in the dark? To be leaving in the dark? To see an open doorway right in front of you and refuse to cross? Sometimes I think I know where you're at, but other times I see plainly that no one can help you find your way. Once I told you a story about a little rabbit who got lost in the forest, but who felt safer when all his little animal friends walked him home. And today, when I looked at all the people in your room, at the nurses and the doctors and even the cleaning ladies, especially the cleaning ladies, I thought, Are we helping to walk you Home, Alex? Are we helping keep you safe until you find your way Home? Or are you so far ahead of us that we'll never catch up? Are you walking alone right now, Alex? Are you scared of the dark?

I would walk with you, if I could, my friend Alex. I would walk for you if only I could. But tonight I am forced to sit with my TV set blaring, half watching *The Honeymooners* and half watching the phone. I used that phone just 10 minutes ago, Alex, to call your nurse, and she tells me you're asleep, your dad by your side and your stuffed camel on your bed. Sometimes, when the pain comes back to hurt you, you squeeze the camel as if stuffed camels were meant to help a boy through his last rounds with cancer. You squeeze tight, and the pain goes away, and then you sleep. "What's keeping him alive?" I say in wonder to the nurse on the phone. "We all thought he'd be gone hours ago!" But your nurse knows your own seven-year-old cure for cancer very well. "He wants to live," she tells me simply. That's it. You want to live.

I never witnessed a fight like this, Alex. I never saw 20 pounds of boy take on a monster. And if you're walking by yourself, Alex, I know now it's for this reason, because the power, like the sickness, is inside of you, only you. I cannot give you a single reason to fight for time. I cannot give you a hug strong enough to melt away tumors. I cannot even give you anything to equal what you've given me. And sometimes, times like tonight, when I'm waiting for a phone call I'd give the whole world to prevent, I wonder if I've ever given you anything at all. I doubt if I've ever given you anything at all. But Alex —

I'd give you life if I could.

Steps

A Short Story

The church is filling.

September sunshine spills on the pews and shadows the yellow-veined Bible by my side. Anticipant crowds weave their way through the room, flinging shrill phrases over their immaculately dressed shoulders. I glance briefly at the priest; he is composed and slightly bored, and his thick hands drop tiredly on his flowing black robe. . . . (And her black-clad form knelt shakily by the grave site, and she smiled at me tremulously as I crouched down beside her. Slowly she traced the dates of Daddy's life, and our universe became a gray slab of chiseled marble. . . .)

Elderly aunts I've never seen before are beaming at me. I recognize Michael's mother as she embraces a relative, and I watch her, my future grandmother, taking wobbly high-heeled steps.

I know about steps.

(She met Michael at a nightclub and her step fell in beside his. They shared martinis and confidences, flirted, and fell in love. And she no longer looked widowed, and I no longer felt calm. That night there was a lift in her step and a tune on her lips. That night I fearfully looked up *stepfather* in my Webster's.)

Michael's mother thrusts me before a large, grinning cousin, who carries a handkerchief and says she always cries at weddings. In animated tones they call to the priest, and

Father Landon laughs at them and they call him a love. (. . . He took me to dinner and he told me he loved her. His eyes were hesitant and he leaned forward eagerly. I felt my grip tighten on the fork's silver tines. I thought of my father and I stood up and stepped away.)

The organist steps before an aging brown console. Multichorded music ushers late-comers to the pews. The hymns quicken in my mind, playing faster and faster; they swirl and crescendo in a whirlwind of breathless notes. . . . (The music blared and she turned off the radio. Her eyes were anguished and the rage within me heaved. Growing, bubbling, the cry burst forward, "How could you *think* of marrying Michael?!")

A thousand Bibles are suspended in midair and the voices behind them are rising in prayer. Rising, rising, resounding in my ears, a thousand voices. . . . (His voice was uncertain and I knew he was vulnerable. He asked me quietly for my friendship and I took pains to refuse him. A thousand times I watched unmercifully as his eyes winced with hurt. . . .)

The long train of her gown sweeps the aisles with her steps. (Stepping, steps, step, stepfather. . . .) A hushed joy falls over the attentive crowd of friends. (He only wants to be friends. Should I try to be friends? He never said father, he said friends, only friends. . . .)

The carpet whispers slowly under the weight of their steps. (Steps can only go forward, never back. You must step from the past, and when you do, can't step back again. . . .)

Father Landon is speaking in a hushed tone. Her face is aglow and beside her, he is smiling. ". . . by the state of New York, I pronounce. . . ." (Webster's pronounces *step-father*, step-fah-ther. "The second mate of one's mother, not biologically related. . . ." "I want to be your friend." "I'm in love with your mother." He only wants to love me. . . . She loves him. . . . Daddy's gone now. . . .)

". . . you husband and wife." The organ strikes in triumph and I watch as they kiss. A thousand relatives surround her, wish her luck, wish her happiness. A thousand relatives stepping brightly in joy. . . .

He is standing by her side, momentarily uncertain. His eyes meet mine shyly, and I know it's time to act. If I turn from him now, I can leave him forever. . . .

My breath comes in spasms, and I hear my heart beat. But when my legs stop shaking, I turn to Michael, and take a step.

8. Poems

Although I now like to write prose best of all, there was a time when my favorite style was poetry. These are some of my favorite poems.

Angels in the Snow
(for my grandfather)

I remember how you looked
   pulling my sled through the snowstorm
   brushing flakes from graying hair
   with a slightly stiffened hand
   and then lying in a drift
   your yellow face against white powder
   flapping thin arthritic wings
   to make me
   angels in the snow.
      I suppose in 1920
      you built snowmen in the meadow
      you were young
      your arms were supple
      the snowmen also knew your touch
And I remember how you looked
   hollow frame in an iron wheelchair
   blue eyes sunk in a mass of wrinkles
   staring blankly into space
   and then I turned to leave the Home
   your trembling hand reached out to touch
         me
   and I kissed the helpless fingers
      that once made
      angels in the snow.

158

Christmas Card
(for the friend who moved)

I know
on a southern coast
you are stringing popcorn
in the heat.
A glass of lemonade stings
steamy fingers, and you
brush sweat with the palms
I once held mittened in the
cold.

Looking through ornaments, you find the
scarf that I bought you.
It is frayed from winters of tripping
through a thick new england
snow.

In a carton in the attic
I will store your Christmas postcard.
It will smell of salty oceans and a palm tree
growing
green.
I will see again the U-Haul
moving southward from december;
finger-treasured ten-page letters
". . . and I hope to see you soon."

Feeling Guilty

Bury him
   with tears of rage
   and cursed thoughts
   of the old blue Ford
   that didn't see
   his wagging tail
Bury him
   with his favorite toy
   your old green ball
   he never was satisfied
   just to play with it in the yard
   he had to chase it that day,
   by a road, near a highway
   by a speeding car. . . .
Bury him
   with the leash
   that you freed him of,
   such a nuisance, let him *run*
   forgetting that cars run, too,
   on screaming hot wheels
   next to which four wobbly paws
   don't stand a chance
Bury him
   with belated apologies and worthless grief
   with a heart of guilt and a mind crushed
   by the knowledge that you could
   have prevented it all — and didn't
Bury your dog,
   and hope that someone else
   doesn't make
   the same mistake.

Sunday Poem, for My Father

we sit in the car at the end
    of stolen sundays
  relieved by the shadows
      of the need for
        false smiles.

in the house we once shared,
  she moves behind curtains:
    you know she is home and
      will not come outside.

awkwardly we embrace on the
    threshold of monday,
  and i peer at you, memorizing
    your once-a-week eyes.

Wedding Poem

When the days are hard to bear
When my inner shadows clutch
I find solace in your care
I find comfort in your touch.

When my spirits thrill to surge
When my world has met its peace
Then your bliss with mine will merge
Then you feed my joy's increase.

For the wonders you have shown
For the insights that you bring
I have gained a heart that's grown
And a self that's taken wing.

Glory, glory that I feel
I can scarce believe you're real
Life with you is so much more
Than the life I knew before.

162

Pain Song

It hurts today.
My pain feels like a knife
that is piercing my heart
but my grief is too thick to cut.
It hurts today.
My eyelids burn
with salty liquid
tears are formed
and sting my cheeks with loss.
It hurts today.
My heart is like a voice
that's lost its power to speak out.
It sings no songs
and tells no tales
and speaks no words
for there is nothing left to say.
It hurts today.
It hurt yesterday, too
I wonder if
it will hurt tomorrow?

The Haven

There is something in the alley that is native
to my soul
Something calming to my being in this
dirt-infested hole
Where the alley cats are crying and the
garbage is a coat
There is something there of me — something
peaceful, calm, remote.

There is something of me written on the old
grafitti-ed walls
From the hollow iron trash cans something of
my childhood calls
Days I spent among the litter when I wanted
to be free
From the outer world's intrusions — when I
needed time to *be*.

The alley sees me rarely now that I am nearly
grown
I no longer have the time to seek a place to be
alone
Yet when outer pressures crowd me, when I
need to be *apart*,
There stirs something of an alley,
half remembered, in my heart.

The Graduate

Touch the silver iron gate
Look at red brick walls once more
I, who've seen them every day,
Will not see them anymore.

See them one last time and turn
Away to hide the sudden tears
Which spray with salt my memories
Of happy golden years.

In Celebration of A Friend

I like.
I like the times together spent
 the secrets shared
 the funny talks we always have.
I like the birthday cards you send
 the teasing smiles that know no end —
 because we're friends.

I smile.
I smile at silly nicknames called
 the private jokes
 the warm advice you always give
I smile at all the care you've shown
 the way you cheer me up by phone —
 when I'm alone.

I know.
I know that people come to change
 that paths diverge
 that joys are often left behind
I know that closeness is a stage.
We'll grow apart. We'll pass, with age.
And so our friendship is a phase. . . .

But how I've loved these days.

Afterward

I cannot write of the future
    yet I know I'll see it bloom
I can't write solely of sunshine
    for my days will know some gloom
I can't write of pouring rainstorms
    for I hope to see the sun
I can't write of brilliant battles
    till I'm positive I've won.

The Year

One year, Grandpa —
   gained five pounds.
   got a brand new
   bike and an A in math.
   The roses bloomed
   right on time
   this summer
   and Terry won his
   soapbox match.
   One year.
Twelve months, Grandpa —
   cooked my first full dinner.
   had an all night, all right
   date with Keith.
   Mama is fighting to
   preserve the parks.
   She says nothing grows in
   Brooklyn
   anymore.
   One year.

One year, Grandpa,
    and the nights are hardest.
    Dreams serenade your
    face in my eyes.
    White hair glimmers
    once more in the darkness
    till I
    wake up.
Years months weeks days seconds, Grandpa.
    A lone tear trickles
    down my cheek,
    wondering
    why sometimes
    I still don't remember
    you're gone
    when it's been
    one year.

In the Heart of Every Man

I know I can't keep living for the ones
　　who died before
But as the years keep passing I find I miss
　　them all the more
They live only in a world of thoughts
　　and memories that I've stored
And I've just begun to see the pain
　　of this world I must explore.
And I wonder if you're with me,
　　if you'll always hold my hand
And I wonder if they're with me,
　　watching me from distant lands
And I wonder if they see me
　　as I care and share and give
For it is with memories of their death
　　that I shout, "I want to live!"
And yet if legacies of love that they
　　have left me through the years
Have helped me love somebody else
　　fill days with warmth and cheers
And if they have helped me laugh once more
　　thinking of their smiling eyes
And if they can bring me comfort
　　find me peace when someone dies
And if they've strengthened my conviction
　　helped me realize life goes on
Then their death is just a fiction
　　for they're never really gone
For through memories and laughter
　　through the words "I understand"
Their spirit lives forever
　　In the heart of every man.

Untitled

The multitudes still swarm
    on Fifth Avenue and I have
noticed no fewer shoppers
    in the plaza.
Movie lines still cover miles
    of concrete and
city congestion is at
    its all-time peak.
How then, can I explain my
    feeling
That sometimes the whole world
    seems empty without you?

Ode to My Ex-Friend

I miss the days of secrets shared
I miss.
   the easy chats
   the quiet talks we always had.
I miss the birthday cards we'd send
Those long phone calls that knew no end —
   when we were friends.

I laugh.
I laugh at distant Barbie dolls
   the nonsense rhymes
   and Nancy Drew.
What happened to our childhood plans
   the lemonade and popcorn stands
   we had before we grew . . .
        apart?

I sigh.
I sigh at thoughts of other ages
   at friendships left on journal pages
   what happened to those best of friends?
   Our life-styles changed. We met an end.
   A distant silence time has brought
   I seldom give you any thought.

But yet, sometimes I miss you much.
And wish that we had kept in touch.

On Cystic Fibrosis

I like to pretend
that it doesn't exist
that it's only a term
in a medical book
or a word to describe
someone else
but not me.

It comes to life though
in the form of a mask
in the mist of a tent
or an ocean of pills
and I'm forced to admit that
it's not just a word
or a term in a book
from which I can flee —
that it's me.

Afterword

Robyn Miller

In her introduction to Chapter Six, Robyn says she felt a "nagging superstition that August was out to get me and my c.f. friends." It is terribly sad to report that August did "get" Robyn Miller. She died on August 7, 1985, just as this book was about to go to press. She was 21.

I cannot write that she "passed away," "left us," "is at peace." I know Robyn would say "die." She was a realist, and she detested euphemisms like "passed away" because they tend to gloss over how tough life can be.

She used the word herself in something she wrote for Scholastic *Voice* magazine: "I'll derive great satisfaction from living to see some of my work published, knowing that I'm leaving something nice behind when I die."

As the editor of *Voice* at the time, I asked her, "Wouldn't you rather say 'when I'm gone' instead of 'when I die'? After all, you leave something behind when you *go* somewhere." She was adamant: It must read "die."

Is this book "something nice"? She dearly hoped so. I was with Robyn the day before she died, and she knew clearly that she had only hours left. One question burned through her thoughts. Unable to speak because she had a respirator tube down her throat, she asked for a pen, and weakly scratched out the question: Will my book be published anyway?

Thanks to the editors, I was able to assure her it would. You are holding in your hands a piece of the heritage that was closest to Robyn's heart in her darkest hour.

Robyn entered Brooklyn's Long Island College Hospital on a Monday. By Wednesday, she suspected that she was in her final illness. In the two weeks that followed, she might have been forgiven for thinking only of herself. She did not.

First, she asked her parents to call those of us she was closest to, and to suggest a visit to the hospital so she could say good-bye. Of course, she never said that was the reason; but she could not leave without letting us know of her love. She was thinking about us, not herself.

In the next days, this came out even more.

For example, in her relationship to her father. In the past four years, when Robyn's illness was at its worst, her father was busy earning the family's living. When Robyn was in the hospital, or being cared for at home, it was her mother who looked after her needs. It was her mother who developed an extraordinary rapport with her child. It was her mother whom Robyn called her hero because she came to the hospital during a blizzard that kept most of the city indoors.

Where did that leave her father? The thought obviously troubled Robyn. During that last hospital stay, Robyn's mother was always close by, helping her or holding her hand. But one morning, Robyn asked, "Where's Daddy? I want to hold *his* hand." In fact, he was right there. She took his hand, and for hours afterward, she didn't let go.

Naturally, she wanted her father's hand to comfort her. But he, and her mother, and the rest of us, all recognized that this request was also something else: It was Robyn's declaration of love to her father.

As mentioned, there came a point in this last illness when Robyn knew she had barely 24 hours left to live. Though her eyes were closed, though she had scarcely the strength to move, her mind was alert. Then her aunt arrived, without "Uncle Carl," her husband, who was ill in another hospital. At once Robyn asked for the pen.

What do you suppose Robyn wrote? Was it "Thank you for visiting me"? Was it "I don't feel good"?

No. It was just two words: "How's Carl?"

So if you feel Robyn's love reaching toward you from the pages of this book, it's no mistake. Robyn felt no pity for herself, even at the end, but she felt bottomless pity for everyone else. And she could put that pity, that love, into words.

Robyn had a rare gift, to make public language speak to the private person. All of us who knew her face to face were aware that we shared her with the thousands of people she reached through her writing.

One teacher wrote to her, "Robyn, I know you'll make it." And Robyn answered, "You're right. I'll win. Even if I die, I'll win, because I've had such a great life. I'm ahead of most people that way. God and I both know how lucky Robyn Miller is."

And God and we all know how lucky we are to have had her.

— Niel Glixon

For more information on cystic fibrosis, or to make donations in Robyn's name, write to the Cystic Fibrosis Foundation, National Office, 6000 Executive Boulevard, Rockville, Maryland 20852.